"Rob and Stephanie have written process of early parenthood that balances out the biblical and practical eminently well. With practical advice flowing out of their biblical convictions, they neither prescribe nor mandate, but offer sage advice for a time in life when most couples desperately need it. This will now replace diapers as my go-to gift for newly expectant parents!"

Jonathan Holmes, Pastor of Counseling, Parkside Church; executive director, Fieldstone Counseling

"As a friend, I've had the privilege of watching the Greens' children thrive under their care. I've also seen the impact of their first book, *Tying the Knot*, as we use it to prepare couples in our church for marriage. This new volume is filled with the same kind of wisdom, grace, and focus on Christ that characterized their first book, so I expect to see God use this just as greatly for his glory."

Brad Bigney, Pastor of Grace Fellowship; ACBC certified counselor; conference speaker; author of *Gospel Treason: Betraying the Gospel with Hidden Idols*

"*Tying Their Shoes*, by Rob and Stephanie Green, offers exactly what the subtitle suggests. It is a Christ-centered approach to preparing for parenting. Don't take that subtitle promise lightly. Some books on parenting provide a broad, Christ-centered approach, but they never address the nitty-gritty details of real-life parenting. Other parenting books talk about a ton of details, but you wonder where the gospel makes a foundational impact. In *Tying Their Shoes*, Rob and Stephanie provide that rare balance: a parenting book that relates gospel reality to daily reality. *Tying Their Shoes* will be my go-to book to recommend to young parents, just as *Tying the Knot* has been the number one book I recommend to engaged couples."

Bob Kellemen, Vice President and Academic Dean, Faith Bible Seminary; author of *Raising Kids in the Way of Grace*

"I find this book to be very helpful for couples who really want to get it right as it relates to parenting from a biblical perspective with the right heart attitude. Rob has a unique way of doing exegesis and exposition so that it connects to the heart of individuals and the issues that need to be addressed. The stories and illustrations are heartfelt and very insightful. This book will help a lot of families."

> **Nicolas Ellen**, Senior Professor of Biblical Counseling, the College of Biblical Studies; senior pastor, Community of Faith Bible Church

"What a book! Rob and Stephanie engagingly apply God's Word to the minute details of pregnancy, labor and delivery, raising babies, marital adjustments, and more. My wife, Lauren, and I commend it as a gospel-driven, hope-giving, refreshingly transparent (we loved their humble admissions of failure), and surprisingly practical biblical guide for every expectant or new parent—and all of us who love them (and are looking for gift ideas)."

> **Robert D. Jones**, The Southern Baptist Theological Seminary; author of *Pursuing Peace* and *Uprooting Anger*

"I would have loved to read this book with my wife prior to the birth of our first child. It's full of practical and wise advice from a godly couple."

> **Andy Naselli**, Associate Professor of New Testament and Theology, Bethlehem College & Seminary; elder, Bethlehem Baptist Church

Tying Their Shoes

Tying Their Shoes

A Christ-Centered Approach
to Preparing for Parenting

Rob and Stephanie Green

New
Growth
Press

WWW.NEWGROWTHPRESS.COM

New Growth Press, Greensboro, NC 27404
www.newgrowthpress.com
Copyright © 2019 by Rob and Stephanie Green

Cover Design: Faceout Books, faceoutstudio.com
Interior Typesetting and eBook: Lisa Parnell, lparnell.com

ISBN: 978-1-948130-61-5 (Print)

ISBN: 978-1-948130-62-2 (eBook)

Library of Congress Cataloging–in–Publication Data on file

Printed in the United States of America

26 25 24 23 22 21 20 19   1 2 3 4 5

Contents

Acknowledgments

THE SUCCESS OF *Tying the Knot* has been a pleasant surprise. So far, God has used it in the lives of mentors, pastors, and those preparing for marriage. We (Rob and Stephanie Green) are very thankful. As we continue to minister to young couples in our church, we are reminded of one resource we longed to have years ago—something that would help us prepare for parenting.

We are thankful for this opportunity to bring the Scripture to bear in a practical way for those who are expecting. We are also thankful to New Growth Press for their work and the expertise that helped produce this work.

When we told one friend about the possibility of writing a book called *Tying Their Shoes*, he suggested that we have an entire series through the stages of life where the final book would be called *Tying Up Loose Ends*. We still laugh about that.

This book will have a similar style to *Tying the Knot*. Stephanie and I hope that our use of Scripture is thoughtful, wise, and exegetically sound. We also hope that we have made that truth easy to understand, winsome, and practical.

We are deeply grateful for our young couples' Adult Bible Fellowship at Faith Church. You have helped us think more carefully about the contents of this book. We have loved serving with you in the ministry of our church and thank you for allowing us to be part of your lives.

Introduction

CONGRATULATIONS! IF YOU are reading this book, you are likely expecting the arrival of a baby into your home very soon. We (Rob and Stephanie Green) are so happy for you. Psalm 127 says, "Behold, children are a heritage from the LORD, the fruit of the womb a reward. . . . Blessed is the man who fills his quiver with them!" (3, 5a). As parents, we know that human life is the greatest of all the stewardship opportunities the Lord gives. Every human life is precious because every human is made in the image of God.

We have the joy of parenting three children.[1] Our oldest child is in college. In a short time he will be on his own. Who knows, maybe our family will grow as a result of his marriage in the near future. It is hard to believe that we are old enough to have a college-aged child. While we still pretend that we are young and strong, we are watching God grow the next generation before our eyes. With each passing year, we see a little less of our generation and a little more of theirs. We rejoice as we watch him, and those like him, fulfill God's plan for their lives. Having an adult child for the first time also means that we are actively learning how to be parents to an adult who is transitioning out of our home.

---

1. We knew about a fourth pregnancy, but we never had the privilege of meeting that child. The birth announcement is still in our garage. After seventeen years it is not in a prominent place, but we cannot bring ourselves to discard it.

Our middle child is in high school. He is active in athletics and with friends. It has been a joy in this season of life to exercise together—even if he lifts more weight than Rob. Our middle son is trying to determine what the Lord wants him to do with his life. This means we are actively discipling a teenager. We have to be intentional with our time because it passes much too quickly.

Our youngest child is entering middle school. Our youngest is also our only daughter, and our days include lots of hugs and butterfly kisses. We love watching her care for her dolls. Her innocence is a true delight. Her smile is still that of a little girl, and her giggles make us laugh after she has gone to bed.

Our children have been a great source of joy, encouragement, growth, and occasionally frustration. Each season of parenting is a great privilege and a high calling from the Lord. Since God makes all people in his image, they are precious in his sight. They are, of course, precious in their parents' sight as well.

Parenting children is a great joy, but parenting is not easy. The transition between a home without children to a home with a child is significant. In fact, it is earthshaking. Two people who are used to caring for themselves bring home a little baby who requires constant care. It is hard to put that experience into words. It is a joyful, terrifying, exciting, and intimidating experience.

As we began our journey we looked for resources that would help Stephanie through the pregnancy and prepare her for labor and delivery. Because Stephanie was a registered nurse, she enjoyed learning what was happening to our baby and her body as she progressed toward delivery. Even though she had been in the delivery room as a nursing student, she was interested to read what she should expect as the patient (medical professionals sometimes make the worst patients). I (Rob) was not equally excited about the medical side. However, we both wanted to know a little about caring for a baby. After all, ready or not, we were going to have a child in our home in a few months.

2

We found resources that advised us regarding sleep habits for both parents and babies, when it would be wise to call a doctor (new parents can be a bit dramatic, even if they were not previously), and the value of regular teaching. These concepts and resources were helpful, but not sufficient.

What we needed to prepare for this transition from the two of us to the three of us was something far more than a guide to pregnancy and a plan to survive infancy (although both were helpful). *We needed to understand how God's grace was going to help us every step of the way. We needed to see God's grace in the days when everything was going according to plan. And we needed to see God's grace when the day was crashing.*

We think this is a good place for you to pause and thank God for the grace he has given to allow your family to grow. (If God's grace sounds new or unusual, appendix B explains the gospel of Jesus Christ and how you can experience the grace of his wonderful salvation.)

Some of you were able to be get pregnant easily. Count this pregnancy as a gift of grace from the Lord. Others of you experienced God's grace while you waited for this day. Praise him for sustaining you through the months when you were not expecting. Now, praise him for the blessing of pregnancy. Praise him that today is the day you can finally read a book about preparing for parenting. Or maybe you are seeing God pour out his grace as you add to your family through adoption. Today is a great day, and we encourage you to praise the Lord for his marvelous grace.

In our case, pregnancy did not come easy. The grace that sustained us during the days of infertility and that brought us a pregnancy was the same grace we would need to steward our bundles of joy. We needed God's grace and the truths of the gospel to penetrate our deepest thoughts, fears, hopes, and expectations. We needed the hope of the death, burial, and resurrection of Christ not only for eternity with the Lord, but also for those moments when our three-week-old would not stop crying. We needed to know how two people with the ability to care for themselves could rely on God's grace to steward this new human life. We wanted to thrive and not just survive.

We had no delusions of grandeur. We knew that parenting would not be easy. We knew that there would be ups and downs and turns in all directions. But what we needed to know was how Jesus Christ and our relationship with him could influence every one of those little moments. We needed to know how Jesus could help us in the good moments—and in the challenging moments.

We needed to have confidence that the Lord was great, powerful, and able. He can make all grace abound to us in order for us to handle the events of each day in a Christlike way. We needed God to be our rock, fortress, and strong deliverer.

Admittedly, we struggled, and we continue to struggle, with knowing how to best respond when we are concerned about something, how to give truth and grace along with consequences that reflect God's wisdom, or how to discern the difference between immaturity and high-handed rebellion. But we also know that we have a God who delights in providing mercy and grace for our time of need (Hebrews 4:16).

We invite you, new parents, on a journey with us. What is written on these pages is something we have lived (in the sense that we welcomed our first child into our home twenty-one years ago) and are living right now as we continue to walk the journey of parenting. This is not esoteric knowledge. It is our prayer that the following pages will show you ways to apply God's truth in your daily life as new parents.

While certain chapters emphasize the husband's or wife's role, we have worked together on all the chapters so that they relate to both husbands and wives. We want to show that God's Word is so wonderful that it speaks to all of us.

We hope that this book serves as the continual pointer to Jesus Christ. We hope that you will enjoy this resource, and we especially hope that God will use his Word, his Spirit, and his people to help you love him, rely on him, and see him as your source of strength in the midst of constant change. We hope that by the time you have finished reading the book, you are so thankful for God's grace that you are ready to enjoy your upcoming parenting journey.

Chapter 1
Identity in Christ and Parenting

THE WORDS *MOM* and *dad* are powerful words. Parents have the opportunity and privilege to care for a child. While babies will not be able to say "mama" or "dada" for a while yet, it will not be long before they look at their mom or dad differently than they look at others. Even before children can say the words, they will communicate the special place their parents have in their heart and life. Sometimes the communication will come in the form of a smile, in the desire to be held, or even in an abrupt end to crying.

As children grow, the words *mom* and *dad* will be audible, and will be a constant reminder that God gave parents a special earthly joy—the joy of being a parent. This is a reason to rejoice. It is a special privilege. As celebration, we encourage parents to take photographs, to write in a journal, or to keep specific traditions.

In the society in which Jesus lived, children were sometimes viewed as a liability and often viewed as a lower member of society. In spite of this cultural norm, Jesus uses children as positive illustrations of faith. He encourages children to come to him and tells adults to come to him as a child does.

In our society, parents sometimes make children the center of their lives. It is possible to be intoxicated by the charms of a new little one and forget some of the more foundational elements of the

Christian life. Parents may view themselves as servants to their children, designed to respond to each request. In other words, parents sometimes find their identity in their child. The word *mom* or *dad* becomes more than a privilege—it becomes an identity, even THE identity.

We encourage new parents not to find their first identity in their children. Being a parent is a wonderful gift, an incredible stewardship, and a source of joy. However, being a parent does not change one's core identity or the source of their inner strength, or the place of stability in their life. Only Jesus Christ can provide those elements.

Therefore, in this chapter we want to expand the ideas of identity, strength, and stability and show how the gospel shapes them. The gospel prepares parents to love their child without allowing their child to change their core identity.

Identity

Our identity is how we think about ourselves. We could give many answers to the question, who are you? We could speak about our vocation. Rob can say that he is a pastor. Stephanie can say she is a registered nurse. Those statements of identity are true. They also explain how we spend a significant amount of our time. But even more than that, our vocation tells another something about how we believe God has gifted us and led us at this stage of our life. We both believed that God led us into our vocation. However, as important as our vocation is in terms of how we spend our time or energy, our vocation does not define us.

In a conversation about identity, we could speak about our family. There are many wonderful truths about our family. We are married. Praise God that in 2018, we celebrated twenty-five years of marriage. Since Stephanie and I have spent twenty-five years together, we are different people than we were when we married. Our union has brought about changes in how we function and how we handle relationships. Marriage has refined our character. We could also speak about each of our children. Our children have enriched our lives, and the identity of parents describes a bit about who we are. Like vocational identities, family identities are significant, and they explain some facts about who we are.

When we think about identity, we could even speak of certain loyalties. Indiana has been our home for the last eighteen years. But those who know us well know that we are fans of Ohio State. We both grew up in Columbus, Ohio. Rob's parents went to Ohio State when Rob was a child. He remembers playing on the oval, walking around campus, and eating ice cream at the Baskin-Robbins on High Street. Rob was a member of the rowing team and graduated from Ohio State. Rob likes to say, "I left my blood, sweat, tears, and my parents' money at Ohio State." Even though we live in Purdue University's backyard, we are Buckeyes. Admittedly, Rob's identity as an Ohio State fan is not as important as his vocation or his family, but it is still part of who he is.

As valuable and important as vocational, family, or other loyalties might be, these identities are not large enough to encompass who we are, and they are not sufficient to carry us through the challenges and trials of life. Our vocational identities could change (and they have in our past); the company we are employed by could downsize or even close. Thus, vocations are not stable enough to help us please God and navigate life successfully. Our family identities could also change (some people have experienced unexpected deaths or unwanted divorce). Those who wrap their identities primarily in their family are crushed when these events occur. And our allegiances can disappoint us. I remember when Ohio State lost to Michigan nine out of ten years. The game always happened around Thanksgiving! We either needed to play better or move the time of year when the game was played. Do you see the danger? If our core identity is our vocation, our family, or an allegiance, we could be very disappointed and discouraged should it fail.

9

These identities are not stable enough or strong enough to support new parents in the midst of trials, difficulties, or fears for the future. Parents need something much better, much stronger, and much more stable. Parents who follow Jesus Christ have it. The Bible explains that believers have a wonderful, strong, and sufficient identity for all that a believer will experience.

Identity in Christ deserves an entire book, but this chapter will concentrate on five answers to the question, who are you in Christ?

1. *You are a child of God.* Paul writes, "In love he predestined us for adoption to himself as sons through Jesus Christ, according to the purpose of his will, to the praise of his glorious grace, with which he has blessed us in the Beloved" (Ephesians 1:4b–6).

Ephesians 1:3–11 is a prayer of thanksgiving for the contribution that the Father, Son, and Spirit make in salvation. It is an encouraging passage that demonstrates the great love of God in drawing his people to himself. Notice the words and phrases like *love, purpose of his will,* and *blessed.* God does not draw people to himself by dragging them against their will. He does not force anyone to become his child.

Instead, God draws people with his love and kindness. It was through the kind intention of his will that he chose his children. God desires to call individuals to himself. God showed his love through the death of Jesus on the cross, so his children would come willingly and happily to his loving arms.

In the days when parenting feels like a blessing, remember that you are a child of the King. And in the days when you feel inadequate or the pain of your own limitations, you can still remember that you are a child of the King. Knowing that you belong to God because of his kind intention will help you as a new parent to prepare for the highs and lows of parenting.

2. *You are redeemed.* Paul writes, "In him we have redemption through his blood, the forgiveness of our trespasses, according to the riches of his grace which he lavished on us" (Ephesians 1:7–8a).

To be redeemed means being paid for or rescued. Since that redemption required the blood of Jesus, it is the wrath of God that had to be appeased. Sin not only separates people from a close relationship with the Father, it also places them in debt to his wrath. That is why the Bible says that the wages of sin is death (Romans 6:23). Sin earns death.

It is encouraging to remember that when Jesus died on the cross, he made a way for the debt caused by sin to be paid. The debt of God's wrath is not something that people can pay—so Jesus paid instead.

This grace was lavished upon those who turn to Jesus. To *lavish* means to pour out in abundance. God's grace is a lavish gift. Most people can tell the difference between gifts that are given in abundance and gifts that are given to appease. One focuses upon the minimum, and the other focuses upon the maximum. I think the concept of doing just enough to get by is easy to understand. A husband, forgetting an important date on the calendar, drives to the store to buy the obligatory card and gift. But his wife probably knows, and he certainly knows, that he is scrambling. Stephanie used to work Christmas Eve at a retail store when she was in high school, and she saw a number of desperate husbands scrambling to avoid a Christmas without gifts. They were doing just enough to get by. When one gives in abundance, the person invests time, energy, thought, and sacrifice. The Lord lavished his grace on his grace upon his people.

Jesus Christ's death resulted in redemption for all who trust in him.

3. *You are forgiven.* Ephesians 1:7 also emphasizes the forgiveness from sin that Jesus secured. The ideas of adoption, redemption, and forgiveness are very close in meaning. They are like looking at

the doctrine of salvation from slightly different perspectives. When a woman receives her engagement ring, she often looks at it to enjoy the beauty presented by each angle. The light reflects a little differently and the vibrancy of the colors change, but it is still the same ring. The gospel is best appreciated when one sees it from many perspectives. It is easy to go about the day not thinking too deeply about forgiveness. However, the more people think about the forgiveness that God has given them, the more they are able to live for him.

Because of God's forgiveness, guilt over something you did or did not do does not have to cripple you. Instead, believers live in the state of God's forgiveness. When they sin, Christians need to acknowledge it and ask the Lord for forgiveness—and they will receive it. New parents might struggle with guilt over perceived bad choices. Remembering God's forgiveness will help them keep their feet firmly planted in Christ so that they can properly respond to the next moment.

God's forgiveness also reminds believers that they are free to forgive others. During pregnancy, spouses may respond to each other in unkind or unthoughtful ways. Husbands might think their wives are orchestrating some emotional roller coaster to make their lives challenging. Wives might act like their husbands should meet all their demands for ice cream, tacos, extra pillows, quiet music, loud music, or other desires. In those moments, spouses can speak harshly to each other. One spouse might ask for forgiveness. Knowing that God forgives and that believers live in a state of forgiveness allows them to forgive others and to meet each moment with a fresh attitude.

4. *You are promised an inheritance.* Paul continues, describing how believers "were sealed with the promised Holy Spirit, who is the guarantee of our inheritance until we acquire possession of it, to the praise of his glory" (Ephesians 1:13b–14).

Hope comes from help that is available today, and the blessings that will come in the future. A believer in Christ is never without hope. A believer can feel like there is no hope when they forget who they are in Christ. When they remember that God has promised an inheritance and the guarantee for that inheritance is the Holy Spirit, there is hope. The Lord did not base the inheritance on human wisdom or works. Instead, God makes and guarantees that promise.

5. *You have been made alive.* Paul explains reconciliation between God and man in Ephesians 2, saying, "And you were dead in the trespasses and sins in which you once walked. . . . But God, being rich in mercy, because of the great love with which he loved us, even when we were dead in our trespasses, made us alive together with Christ" (Ephesians 2:1–2a, 4–5).

In order for people to be reconciled to God, they have to be made alive. People need God to breathe spiritual life into them.

Dear friends, caring for a new baby and raising a child in the teaching and discipline of the Lord is not easy. It is joyful, but difficult. There are days before the child is born when you might feel inadequate. There are days you might wonder whether you are ready. After the baby is born, you may wonder whether you are doing everything right. There will be moments when you are unsure. It is even possible that you might react in surprisingly hurtful ways in moments of frustration.

Finding your identity in Christ will help you rest in the glorious gospel. It will help you thank the Lord for his adoption, redemption, forgiveness, inheritance, and regeneration. It will help you to pray knowing that you need the Lord and his help for every step of your journey. Finding your identity in Christ will encourage you to ask questions like the following: Am I doing my very best for Jesus by his grace? Am I living out my identity in Christ in this moment? Am I acting on what Jesus has already told me or am I trying to prove my worth? When you are confident that you are free in Christ, then you can rest in him, trust in him, and rely on him in all the little moments of life.

We hope it is clear that while the identity of being mom or dad is a true delight and privilege, it is not stable or strong enough to sustain you through the blessings or the challenges of raising a child. New parents need Jesus for their stability and significance.

You might wonder whether reflecting on our identity in Christ provides the answer to what we should do in a specific situation. While it may not give us a textbook set of answers, it will put us in the right mind-set to be a humble servant before the Lord, seeking his guidance and help.

Knowledge and Power

Ephesians 1—3 helps believers understand their identity in Christ so that they are in the best position to live out the commands of Ephesians 4—6. Paul repeatedly prays during his discussion of identity. Ephesians 1:3–14 is a prayer of thanksgiving; Ephesians 1:15–23 is a prayer for knowledge; Ephesians 3:1, 14–21 is a prayer for power. In the first three chapters, outside of the greeting, only Ephesians 2 and Ephesians 3:2–13 are not prayers.

When Paul outlines what believers need to do (Ephesians 4—6), he emphasizes a lot of praying (Ephesians 1—3). Believers know how to function by living dependently on the Lord through prayer. While this book is written primarily for married couples who are welcoming their first child into the home, the following truths will be revisited many, many, many times throughout the parenting life. Here are a few requests from Ephesians 1—3 that believers should be praying today.

1. Knowledge about God

Paul prays "that the God of our Lord Jesus Christ, the Father of glory, may give you the Spirit of wisdom and of revelation in the knowledge of him" (Ephesians 1:17).

Knowing more about God helps people understand his greatness. His sovereignty comforts believers because they know he is in control. God's presence comforts Christians because they are never alone. His ability to heal the sick, cast out demons, and raise the dead reminds Christians of their ultimate hope. God ensures that temptations are not more than believers can handle with his help (1 Corinthians 10:13). The more believers learn that God is characterized by covenant love, grace, and compassion, the more they are reminded that God cares for them and provides what they need most. Knowledge of God breeds confidence to do what he has commanded.

2. Self-Knowledge

Paul continues his prayer, "having the eyes of your hearts enlightened, that you may know what is the hope to which he has called you, what are the riches of his glorious inheritance in the saints" (Ephesians 1:18).

Believers also need help thinking about themselves properly. It is so easy to either think too much of oneself (I am awesome!) or to think too little (I am horrible!). Paul's prayer request is for believers to know how God actually sees them. I (Rob) will speak for myself. I need God's help to see myself the way God sees me. Left to my own devices, I am tempted to think of myself according to the moment. If today is good, I am good; if today is not good, neither am I. Thankfully, the Lord allows me to reflect on how he sees me.

3. Knowledge of God's Power Working

Paul concludes this prayer saying, "and what is the immeasurable greatness of his power toward us who believe, according to the working of his great might that he worked in Christ when he raised him from the dead and seated him at his right hand in the heavenly places" (Ephesians 1:19–20).

The power that works in the life of a Christian is the same power that raised Christ from the dead and seated him at the Father's right hand. Of all the powers seen in the world, the power to raise someone from the dead is the strongest. Nonetheless, Christians can forget this power. They can look at specific circumstances and assume that things will not change. They can despair when they do not see God working in the way they want him to. Remembering Christ's resurrection power gives believers hope.

Understanding more about God, how he sees us, and his power, leads us to request his power. In Ephesians 3, Paul outlines two ways that God's power can change the lives of believers.

First, Paul prays asking that "he may grant you to be strengthened with power through his Spirit in your inner being, so that Christ may dwell in your hearts through faith" (Ephesians 3:16b–17a).

This is a request that God's power would result in spiritual growth. Imagine purchasing a new home. Even in a custom-build, the house will not have all the personal touches that make it a home. Over time, homeowners add paint colors, decorations, bed coverings, dishes, and pictures. Even the minor dings in the walls make it feel like home. Since our boys are older now, play wrestling normally ends in damaged or broken things. There is a small dent in our oven from one such match, and two doors are bent ever so slightly inward. Those things, while needing to be repaired if we move, are reminders that we are home. On occasion the sight of one such ding results in a comment like, "Dad, do you remember when your face hit those doors and bent them?" "Yes, son, I remember." As believers grow and mature, Christ makes his home continually more comfortable in their hearts.

Parents need Christ to dwell in their hearts. Anger often tempts parents. Fatigue can lead to complaining, especially after a long night. The difficulty of Sunday mornings may tempt some parents to abandon Christian community. As believers grow, they will be able to see these situations differently and respond differently because Christ is granting them inner strength each day.

Secondly, Paul prays for the power to understand the love of God, asking "that you, being rooted and grounded in love, may have strength to comprehend with all the saints what is the breadth and length and height and depth, and to know the love of Christ that surpasses knowledge, that you may be filled with all the fullness of God" (Ephesians 3:17b–19).

Believers are rooted and grounded in God's love. However, there is far more to comprehend. Because God's love is limitless, Christians never stop learning. Others can help. Spouses can talk about God's love together. Active participation in a local church can help too.

When parents lean on Christ's power, the conversations spouses have with each other will be more gospel centered. When parents rely on the knowledge of God, they will be in the right position to make wise decisions. They can provide quality care for their child and for one another. No book can tell parents exactly what is happening when their child is crying in the middle of the night, but we know that as parents rely on the Lord's power working in them, the decisions at two o'clock in the morning about how to respond to their child will be more thoughtful.

Stability

The gospel of Jesus Christ provides stability. Believers know what the Lord has done for them, and they know that knowledge and power are accessible to them. These truths provide a stable foundation. Life can feel chaotic, but when believers control their heart and mind by reflecting on the gospel, then they know they have help. As the psalmist explained, "From where does my help come? My help comes from the LORD, who made heaven and earth. He will not let your foot be moved; he who keeps you will not slumber" (Psalm 121:1b–3). That is a great promise at two o'clock in the morning when it seems like everyone else is sleeping.

17

Change brings instability. Instability brings fear. It can be scary to be pregnant, to have a child, to be a parent. There are many unknowns, but the Lord Jesus who died for his people, who intercedes for them, who gave them his Holy Spirit, will not abandon you in parenthood. The Lord Jesus will always be a rock, a fortress, a strong tower, and a great deliverer. When you reflect on your identity, the accessibility of knowledge and power, and the security Christ brings by being with you, you will be in the best position to respond to what the Lord allows in your life.

Exercises

1. Complete the following sentence with the ten words that you believe best fit: I am _____. Then, look for a passage of Scripture that would support your statement (For example, I am forgiven [Ephesians 1:7]).

2. Pray with your spouse three times this week. Ask that God would help you understand more fully who he is, who you are, and the depth of his power, and that this would fill you with confidence and peace as you await this big life change.

3. Pray with your spouse three times this week, and ask that you would notice God exercising his power in your life. Ask him to grow you and make you more like Christ. Ask him to help you understand aspects of his love that you have never seen before.

4. Since this chapter is a foundation for all that comes later, discuss weekly as a couple your identity statements, the things God is teaching you, and the ways you are seeing God's power displayed in your life. Consider posting a couple passages of Scripture in the nursery so you can easily refer to these truths.

Chapter 2

Help Your
New Baby by Prioritizing
Your Marriage

ADDING A FAMILY member to the home is very exciting. It is easy to think of the joys that the new bundle of life will bring. We believe it is good and right for expecting parents to be excited. We also believe the marriage relationship comes first. Preparation for a baby needs to involve strengthening the relationship between spouses.

Parents naturally want to care for their new baby. However, those who place the baby at the center of their existence create distance in their marriage that will in the long run negatively affect their lives with each other, their children, and their relationship with God. Strong marriages, with Christ at the center, welcome a child into a home that is functioning according to gospel priorities. Children growing up in these kinds of homes experience many blessings. We will provide a few ideas on how parents can prioritize their marriage while preparing for their baby's arrival.

We realize that many children are not born to married parents. Sometimes the relationship between the biological parents collapses long before the due date. If you are in that situation, God can give you the grace needed to raise your child. Single parents can still follow much of the advice in this book. This chapter about marriage and the ones involving fathers/mothers can help you wisely select a spouse, should that day come. We encourage you to use this book, and books like it, to help you decide whom to marry.[2]

Perhaps you and the baby's other parent are living together, but not legally married. We strongly encourage you to speak to your pastor and receive individual advice. Those living together can benefit from this book, but relationship dynamics will have an important impact on building the foundation of your life on Christ.

This chapter will consider two passages of Scripture, Genesis 2:18–24 and Ephesians 4:1—6:4.

> Then the LORD God said, "It is not good that the man
> should be alone; I will make him a helper fit for him."
> Now out of the ground the LORD God had formed
> every beast of the field and every bird of the heavens
> and brought them to the man to see what he would
> call them. And whatever the man called every living
> creature, that was its name. The man gave names to all
> livestock and to the birds of the heavens and to every
> beast of the field. But for Adam there was not found a
> helper fit for him. So the LORD God caused a deep sleep
> to fall upon the man, and while he slept took one of his
> ribs and closed up its place with flesh. And the rib that
> the LORD God had taken from the man he made into a
> woman and brought her to the man. Then the man said,
>> "This at last is bone of my bones
>> and flesh of my flesh;
>> she shall be called Woman,
>> because she was taken out of Man."

2. You may benefit from Rob's earlier book, *Tying the Knot* (Greensboro, NC: New Growth Press, 2016) or from Ernie Baker's work titled *Marry Wisely, Marry Well* (Wapwallopen, PA: Shepherd Press, 2016).

Therefore a man shall leave his father and his mother
and hold fast to his wife, and they shall become one
flesh. (Genesis 2:18–24)

God designed a marriage and procreative plan that involved a
woman and a man made in God's image. A man leaves his parents
and cleaves to his wife, and the two become one flesh.

Genesis 2:18–24 teaches about the priority of marriage. In a
home, children will leave, but the marriage remains. Adam and Eve
marry and have children. Their children then marry. Children leave
their homes to establish a new home with a new marriage and a new
family. Yet, because marriage is designed to last a lifetime, the marriage remains intact after the children leave home.

Since God intends marriage to last a lifetime, he commands
parents to cultivate a strong and Christ-centered marriage. In that
place of strength, parents can welcome little ones into their home.
The children are important, but not all-important.

This same mentality can also be found in Ephesians 4—6 where
Paul emphasizes believers' relationships within the church, within
their marriages, and as parents. After the call to live worthy lives of
the gospel (Ephesians 4:1), the Lord provides many ways for a person
to practically live that way. Ephesians 4:2-6 provide some foundational elements of the Christian life, like keeping unity through
humility, gentleness, and patience. Unity in the church requires
those elements, but so does unity in the home. If spouses argue and
grow bitter against one another by holding on to their own ways of
doing things, then it will be very easy for a child to divide them.

Ephesians 4:7-16 emphasizes the role of service in the church
and using God-given gifts and abilities to build up the body in love.
Part of living a gospel-centered life is actively contributing to the
ministry. Some will be teachers; others will be leaders; others will
be shepherds; others will serve behind the scenes. Rather than let
a marriage or a child stand in the way of that, God-honoring and

Christ-loving followers will continue to find ways to build up the body in love.

Those who live worthy of the gospel know that they need to grow in their Christian walk and are committed to doing so (Ephesians 4:17–32). Change is difficult. It requires the work of the Spirit and a commitment to invest time and energy. For example, learning to solve problems quickly (Ephesians 4:26–27) sounds good, but is not so easy. Life's transition periods, like welcoming a new baby, can pose particular challenges. Just as parents had to transition to living with a new spouse, so they will also have to transition to living with a baby. These life changes have a way of exposing new ways believers need to become selfless.

In Ephesians 5:2, walking worthy of the gospel involves living a life of love and avoiding being a person characterized by immorality, impurity, greed, or filthy speech. These sinful patterns must be exposed and changed (Ephesians 5:6–14) rather than indulged.

This portion of Ephesians explains that godly people walk wisely (Ephesians 5:15) and are filled by the Spirit (Ephesians 5:18–21). Ephesians 4:2—5:21 emphasizes a series of ways that a person must be first committed to Christ.

Ephesians 5:22–33 outlines how those who live worthy of Christ also fulfill certain responsibilities in the marriage. Wives are to submit to their husbands and husbands are to love their wives like Christ loved the church. The marriage is to be a gospel witness of the relationship between Christ and the church. Verse 33 reiterates the tasks of love and respect.

These ideas should be in place when parents bring a little one in the home.[3] Those marriages that have not established these roles in

---

3. If your marriage is struggling, then we encourage you to take some action right away. First, stop reading this book. You can come back to it. Second, either go through a marriage resource like *This Momentary Marriage* by John Piper, or *Strengthening Your Marriage* by Wayne Mack, or even a premarital resource (like *Tying the Knot*) to be sure that you are working on your marriage. Third, if a book will not be sufficient to correct the problems, then we encourage you to contact your pastor for personal help.

advance will find that they impact how they parent—even early on in the process. A husband unwilling to lead before a child may find leadership even more difficult to exercise after a baby. A wife who does not respect or submit to her husband will not find it easier in the midst of caring for an infant.

Ephesians 6:1–4 emphasizes the parent-child relationship, following an emphasis on relationships in the church and marriage. Children must obey their parents, and parents— fathers in particular—must bring them up rather than provoke them.

The late seminary professor Dr. Bill Arp once explained to our Sunday school class that there is a pattern from Ephesians 4 through 6. God first outlines what it looks like to walk worthy of the gospel as a person. Then God outlines what it looks like to walk worthy as partners. Then God outlines how to walk worthy as parents. In our ministry, we have seen people who were not first committed to Christ welcome children into their home. We have seen people welcome little ones who were not functioning well as a married couple. In these situations, they did not develop Christ-centered or gospel-centered homes.

Marriage comes before parenting. While there will be seasons of life when it seems like the children are dominating everything (like the first few weeks), parents must remember that their marriage is one of the foundational elements of the home. What are the practical reasons why your relationship with Christ and your marriage come before your child?

Reason #1: The strength to handle difficult moments

It would be nice if every day went exactly as we hoped. That is not always the case. Imagine a difficult day with work being stressful, long, and hard. It seemed that your boss was upset with you, a deadline was quickly approaching, and so many people interrupted you that it was six in the evening before you finally started on *your* work. You come home tired and emotionally spent. Then imagine that your child is also having a very rough day. Your baby is not sleeping well or eating well. Since your baby is tired, he or she is fussy and to the point where nothing satisfies him. Everyone— mom, dad, and baby—is stressed, emotionally spent, and wanting to rest. But rest does not come. It will be long night.

Those who have children can remember days like this. Reminders of gospel truths and both parents working together get them through these moments in a Christ-centered way. Let's focus on working together, since the last chapter focused on gospel truths. After attempting to console, comfort, and provide for your baby, you start expressing your frustration. It comes out in body language, or the way you walk around the room, or the way you speak. That signals that the best course of action is to lovingly and gently remind one another of Scripture, the passages you hung around the nursery, and the importance of changing responsibilities. It might be time to put the child down or to have the other spouse hold him or her while you rest.

Part of the strength Christ gives to his people is the strength that comes from leaning on each other. When one is weak the other is there to lift him up, as Solomon explains, "Two are better than one, because they have a good reward for their toil. For if they fall, one will lift up his fellow. But woe to him who is alone when he falls and has not another to lift him up!" (Ecclesiastes 4:9–10).

Reason #2: The wisdom to know what to do and say

Parenting an infant, as you know, has stressful moments. Sometimes God will give strength to you through the thoughtful and godly advice of your spouse. The same is true for the use of your tongue. Wisdom flows from a heart that is fixed on Christ; it flows from a desire to truly love one another; and it flows as we lovingly correct one another's attitude.

Since Rob was in seminary when our first child was born, there were times that Stephanie took an extra load to allow him to finish a paper or prepare for an exam. There were other times when Stephanie benefited from a couple hours out of the house. Learning to work together well will allow you to have these conversations without anyone being frustrated or feeling neglected.

Reason #3: The ability to establish a consistent united front in parenting through partnership

When you learn to work together as a team in the early days of your parenting, you establish a united front. We have all been in the grocery store and watched one parent tell their child no to a request, only to see the other parent fulfill it. We have seen parents whose toddlers argue until they get their way. While the toddler is responsible for his or her actions, the groundwork for these moments happened while their baby was in the nursery. The parents established a pattern where each did his or her own thing. They did not parent as a united front. It did not take long for the child to learn that and take advantage of it.

We encourage you to communicate and use the God-given roles to establish a parenting plan you agree on as a couple. Stick to that agreement until the two of you establish a different course of action. For example, let's say that a couple agrees that normal solid food will be introduced in stages. However, dad and the baby go to the store to purchase a few items and there is a small sample of ice cream. Surely this will not hurt. Our baby will not choke, he reasons. Here is the problem—Mom and Dad had an agreement! This example may seem small, but it sows seeds that could lead to discord. Other times Dad may have asked Mom to please not violate the approach they are taking to their child grabbing eyeglasses. Yet, Mom chooses not to keep that approach when Dad is not watching. These are not just parenting issues, they are marriage issues.

Reason #4: The ability to understand your child a little easier by working together

Raising a person is a long, and sometimes difficult, process. Each child is an independent person with unique gifts and abilities. Each child has his or her own personality. Each child will develop his or her own desires and idols of the heart. It is not always easy to understand what is motivating a child to think, to love, and to behave in certain ways. Each day, parents are learning about their children. How does a child learn best? How can parents help their children use their abilities for the Lord? Is anything in their life more important than Jesus? These questions are easy to ask and hard to answer. When a couple has a strong marriage, they both work together to answer those questions. Together, they develop plans to help the child, and they support one another in the process.

A Word about Expectations

Some parents believe that a child will make their relationship stronger. Rarely is that the case. Children, even little ones, bring their own personalities, abilities, and desires to the family. That means that children can create conflict rather than solve it. We encourage you to recognize that parents who are seeking to honor Christ as individuals and as a couple are in a much better position to receive a child with joy.

Some parents believe that their children will have the same sets of gifts and abilities as the parents. There are some children who are clearly like one of their parents. However, we believe that God gives every child a set of gifts and abilities and a set of limitations. Rob, for example, will never run a sub 4:00 mile. There is no amount of time, diet, or training that will overcome that physical limitation. Nor will Rob dunk a basketball. These are all limitations.

Stephanie, on the other hand, is far more gifted athletically, but being a nuclear physicist was not part of God's plan for her. There were some limitations that were tailored to her. Every child is a gift from the Lord and has their own set of gifts and limitations. Look for the unique traits God has gifted your child with. Do not expect them to be just like you; celebrate how God has made them. Even as you wait for the day your baby is born, pray and ask the Lord to help you celebrate how he has gifted your little one. Pray that you would find joy as you learn their gifts, skills, and abilities.

Some expecting parents request prayer that their child will be physically healthy. While requesting a healthy child can be similar to a request for a successful surgery, or a job offer, or a quick labor and delivery, it is important that parents pray this with some things in mind.

First, that we always pray according to the Lord's will (James 4:15). We know that the Lord is gracious in giving us a life, made in the image of God, to steward. That is a privilege regardless of how the Lord has equipped our child.

Second, requests for healthy babies must be placed in the right context. Those who have children with special needs love their children. They love their gifts and abilities. They love the contributions they make to their family dynamics. They would not trade their children for the world. As a result, requests for health can sometimes sound insensitive to those around whose children might not have complete physical and mental health. There is a balance here.

We encourage you as couples to pray for your unborn children. You can pray for the doctors, the labor and delivery process, and the health of your child, but also remember to pray as the Lord wills, believing that God will give grace for whatever gift/limitation package your child has.

Potential Ways to Build Unity Prior to a New Arrival

Unity is crucial in the church and in your marriage. The stronger a marriage union, the more ready you will be for your baby. You can build unity in marriage in many different ways. Here are a few ideas to get started.

Build Unity through Shared Commitments

Every couple has to agree about certain things before they are able to live in unity. As we look back, we realize that we avoided many arguments about certain subjects because we agreed about them.

For example, Stephanie and I grew up as savers, rather than spenders. While each of us spent money on a few things, we largely believed that we had what we needed and tried to save what we could. After we married, those patterns remained. When our first child arrived, there was a clear pattern for how we used money. This mutual commitment with our finances allowed us to avoid arguments and live in harmony.

We also agreed that Stephanie would decide whether she nursed our children. Although her decision would affect me (since using formula would change our finances and impact my involvement during feeding times), we still agreed that Stephanie would decide whether nursing would work. Having a shared commitment about these decisions kept us on the same page.

In addition, we agreed before our child was born that it would be best for Stephanie to remain home full-time. This is often one of the more significant decisions to be made. Since we had common ground, it was not something that we argued about.

We believe it is wise to have these conversations before a child is born. We think having shared commitments about important matters will greatly improve your unity and allow you to concentrate on things that will honor the Lord.

Build Unity through Care and Sensitivity

Married couples have to learn to care about one another. They have to learn to be sensitive to one another. It takes time to learn how to do that. We are speaking about the little moments of life and not just the major holidays. Some things are pretty obvious, but others are more nuanced.

In our first year of marriage Stephanie was in nursing school. Rob learned that one way to care for Stephanie was to help her with her homework. Rob could not help her take a blood pressure or start an IV. He could, however, quiz her on her flashcards in preparation for a test or help her with math calculations to be sure she would give a correct dosage. This was one small way that our marriage grew stronger before children arrived. Being sensitive to the challenge of schooling was part of how Rob showed genuine care.

Care flowed in both directions. We were young, still students, and making ends meet as we could. I (Rob) worked three part-time jobs while finishing my last quarter of a physics degree. Stephanie cared for me by packing lunch and dinner because there wasn't time to go home between school and work. Her gesture took less than ten minutes a day, but part of how she cared was to ensure that I was well fed.

Each couple has to determine what care and sensitivity will look like in their relationship. If you have not established these patterns, then we would encourage you to begin right away.

Build Unity through Prayer

We are taught to pray in Matthew 6:9–13, and we are commanded to pray numerous times in the New Testament, including 1 Thessalonians 5:17. In Psalm 13:3, David prays despite feelings of aloneness and abandonment by the Lord. There is hardly a circumstance that is not addressed by prayer. Maybe that is why we find so many prayers in the New Testament and so many calls to pray without ceasing (Colossians 4:2). It is possible to develop a godless self-sufficiency and neglect the importance of prayer as an individual and as a couple. Praying together builds unity because you are both confessing your need. Rather than being the person with all the answers, you are asking for wisdom. The more that you as a couple bathe your new opportunities in prayer, the more unified you will be in the answers God provides and in the questions that still need to be answered.

Build Unity through Fun

We encourage couples to have fun together. You can decide what constitutes fun, but part of being ready for a baby is being encouraged in your own relationship. We used to go to the basketball court at our apartment complex and play a game of H-O-R-S-E with the loser responsible to buy Dairy Queen treats. We were able to join friendly competition with our love for ice cream. Since we combined our finances, it did not matter who paid, only who won.

In fact, competitions were often great sources of fun. In our younger married days, Putt-Putt had a special on Saturday morning-unlimited play from nine in the morning until one in the afternoon with a hot dog and drink for five dollars. Of course, we had to discover who won the most the games, who had the best average score for the day, and who got the lowest score in a single game. Even today, some twenty-five years later, we still talk about our Saturday morning Putt-Putt dates. We found moments like this refreshing, encouraging, and relationship building.

When children came along, there was a culture of fun in our relationship. We were not two people living in war, trying to make peace through a child. As a result, after our first child was born, we often went together to places as ordinary as the grocery store. Admittedly, the grocery store was not as exciting as Dairy Queen, but it became part of our culture of fun. Moments like this helped us remember that we were on the same team in our parenting. When we were tempted to complain about each other, regular fun helped us quickly repent from mean and unhelpful comments.

We encourage you to let the Scripture set the priorities of the heart. A marriage relationship takes priority over the relationships of parents with their children. Welcome God's gift into a world where God is first, the marriage is second, and children are third. Develop unity so that the structure of the home is solid. Right priorities lay the foundation for the joy of parenting.

Exercises

1. Make a list of the five most significant ways you are currently developing unity in your marriage.

2. Make a list of two things you would like to start doing that would strengthen your union.

3. Pray with your spouse three times weekly, asking that God would help you both keep Christ first and each other second. Pray that you would truly cleave to one another physically and emotionally.

4. Do one fun activity this week with your spouse and commit to growing in unity as you wait for your little one to arrive.

Chapter 3

The Lord
Is My Shepherd—
Labor and Delivery

YOUR RELATIONSHIP WITH Jesus and your spouse lay the foundation for godly parenting, but the practical details of parenting are still important. This chapter will focus on labor and delivery. There are many different emotions you might experience during pregnancy. On the one hand, there is excitement as you eagerly await the arrival of your little one. However, as the due date draws closer, the excitement may be accompanied by moments of fear and anxiety.

The thought of labor and delivery can be terrifying, especially with a first baby. During Stephanie's first pregnancy, she remembers looking at mothers and thinking, *She's had a baby and survived. It must not be that bad.* That thought only temporarily calmed her anxious heart. It did not take long for the terrifying fears of the unknown to take up residence once again.

Then came the childbirth classes. We laughed a lot during those classes. The classes were not designed to be funny, but some of the things we were asked to practice in order to be ready for labor were hilarious. However, one class was a little more frightful than fun.

The staff believed it would be helpful to see a video of a woman giving birth. The video amplified Stephanie's anxiety. Stephanie is a nurse who had seen labor and delivery previously. But there was something about seeing this video as a soon-to-be first-time mom that made her nervous.

The upcoming birth became most real during the tour of the hospital. We saw the newborn nursery. There were precious little babies wrapped snugly in their blankets with tiny hats on their heads, sleeping so peacefully in their cribs. If this scene did not get us excited about meeting our baby, we didn't know what would. However, seeing the room where labor, delivery, and recovery occur reminded us that there was some work before we could meet our precious baby. For Stephanie, seeing a labor and delivery room was helpful in making one unknown known prior to labor. However, picturing herself in that bed was a little unnerving.

The days leading up to the due date can be a mixed bag. One moment expectant parents may be excited; the next moment they may be scared. One moment expectant parents may feel ready; the next moment, they may not. The one thing parents know for sure is that the day is coming when this baby will enter the world. As the day approaches, family, friends, and even strangers offer advice. Some even feel the need to share their own experiences of childbirth, which may leave new parents overwhelmed and anxious as the day approaches.

Stephanie remembers the events surrounding our second son's birth. Rob had recently completed his internship for his MDiv and graduated from seminary. With seven weeks left in her pregnancy, we moved to a new home in a new town in order to begin our first ministry after graduation.

One of the first projects we tackled at our new home was remodeling the room that was going to be the nursery—as the due date was fast approaching. After two weeks of diligent work, the nursery was complete. The drywall was finished, the trim was hung, and the walls were painted. The only things left to do were assemble the crib and put up a few decorations—reasonable tasks to complete within the upcoming five weeks.

On a beautiful Sunday evening, Rob had already put in a full day of ministry, and we were still trying to unpack our new home. The only thing Stephanie really wanted to accomplish that evening was assembling the crib. Even though our due date was five weeks away, she really wanted to finish the nursery that night. We put the crib together, and we were ready for the baby . . . at least as far as it having a place to sleep.

We climbed into bed around eleven at night. We were exhausted, but also excited that we had accomplished so much in the first two weeks of living in our new home. We had hope that we were actually going to be ready for our baby's arrival in five weeks.

However, God had other plans. Within thirty minutes of being in bed, Stephanie's water broke. Suddenly, we were not ready at all. There were boxes that still needed to be unpacked, a hospital bag to pack, pajamas to be found, and film to be bought (yes, film). Our two on-call friends who planned to stay with our child while we went to the hospital were both out of town. The nearest family was three and a half hours away.

There were several unknowns associated with having a baby at thirty-five weeks. We were already informed that a team of medical professionals from NICU would be in the room during delivery just in case they were needed. We were thankful for the opportunity to have this kind of medical care, but it also impressed upon us the seriousness of the situation.

As I (Stephanie) lay in a hospital bed during the remainder of that night and the following morning, my heart was a mixed bag of excitement, fear, and anxiety. As you eagerly await the birth of your baby, do you find yourself at times feeling overwhelmed, fearful, or anxious? I sure did, and I am guessing I'm not alone. Let me encourage you to view labor and delivery through the lens of

Psalm 23. As I lay in that hospital bed waiting for our second son to be born, I quietly recited parts of Psalm 23 to myself. At the time, I did not realize the richness or depth of the words I was quoting. Nonetheless, those words were an encouragement to my restless soul.

> The LORD is my shepherd; I shall not want.
> He makes me lie down in green pastures.
> He leads me beside still waters.
> He restores my soul.
> He leads me in paths of righteousness for his name's sake.
>
> Even though I walk through the valley of the shadow of death,
> I will fear no evil, for you are with me;
> your rod and your staff, they comfort me.
> You prepare a table before me in the presence of my enemies;
> you anoint my head with oil;
> my cup overflows.
> Surely goodness and mercy shall follow me all the days of my life,
> and I shall dwell in the house of the LORD forever.

This psalm begins with the Lord being described as my Shepherd. A shepherd is a person who tends, looks after, or cares for sheep. Shepherds protect their flock, at times risking their very life for the sheep's well-being. David's life illustrates this as he tended to his master's sheep. When a lion or a bear carried off a sheep from the flock, David struck the predator and rescued the sheep. Even when a lion or bear turned on David, he killed it (1 Samuel 17:34–35).

Just as shepherds look after, care for, lead, and protect their sheep, so the Lord looks after, cares for, leads, and protects those who follow him. In fact, many places in Scripture use the word *shepherd* to describe Jesus. Jesus is the Good Shepherd (John 10:11, 14), the Great Shepherd (Hebrews 13:20), and the Chief Shepherd (1 Peter 5:4). The Lord has no interest in abandoning his shepherd role in the midst of pregnancy, labor, and delivery. Instead, God's love and care may be experienced in new and surprising ways.

Psalm 23 offers much hope for the day of labor and delivery. Think about the following points and how those might apply to your labor and delivery.

The Lord Is My Shepherd—I Am Protected and Secure

Rest is a major theme in the Bible. Sometimes rest means that one cease from a particular activity. Rest also can be a symbol of provision, protection, and security. Jesus taught the weary and burdened to come to him so he could give them rest (Matthew 11:28–30). The rest that Jesus provided was not sleep but protection, security, and provision for this life and the next.

When Rob was sick as a young child, feeling pain and suffering, his mom would occasionally lay beside him. Somehow, in some way, her presence made him feel secure and comforted, and he would see his physical struggles in a different context. Before his mom came in the room, he was restless with his pain from coughing and sneezing. But once she was there he started to relax and rest. He was not suffering alone. He was suffering in the presence of someone who cared.

Having worked in a hospital for eleven years and experienced labor and delivery three times, I (Stephanie) can tell you that no two labor and delivery stories are exactly the same. Labor and delivery does not follow a cookie-cutter pattern. New moms can easily try to find rest or security in the areas where they have control rather than in a God who cares deeply for them. The best rest is found in the presence of one who cares.

For example, some expectant parents attempt to find rest by attending every class offered on labor, delivery, and newborn care. Taking classes and being prepared can be fantastic. In fact, postpartum nurses love it when their patients confidently care for their infant after birth. However, new parents cannot find their rest in knowledge from classes.

Other expectant parents spend hours on the internet researching articles in order to make a perfect birth plan. While there is nothing inherently wrong with a birth plan, the problem can come when someone's plan for the birth does not match God's. I (Stephanie) have seen it happen several times. A mom comes in with her plan and is adamant that the doctor and nurses follow her plan. When the safety of the baby and/or mom requires a deviation from that plan, it can leave the mom feeling anxious, overwhelmed, and angry. The perfect labor and delivery plan cannot provide safety and security. The Good Shepherd's plan can.

Some attempt to find their rest by choosing the best doctor. Like many, we handpicked our doctor, one who had delivered many babies, performed many surgeries, and faced many emergency situations. The doctor we chose was not only a knowledgeable man, but he was also a godly man who cared for us well. We loved him and were thankful for the opportunity we had to receive such excellent care, recognizing that this was not the case in many parts of the world. But even the best doctors cannot give new parents complete safety and security. Every doctor is human, created by the Creator. Instead, new parents can rest in the fact that whatever happens during labor and delivery happens because God, who cares for them deeply, permits it to happen.

Dads, this is for you as well. Labor and delivery is one of those times that you realize you are not in control. No one is even asking for your advice. This can bring some insecurity. Will my wife be okay? Are others doing what they need to be doing? In these moments, you too can rest knowing that you are protected and secure and that God is actively involved.

As you prepare for the upcoming birth of your baby, what is the basis of your security? Is it in the areas you feel you have control over, or is it in the One who has ultimate control and cares deeply for you? The One who has promised never to leave or forsake you. The One whose love can never be separated from you. Let me encourage you to cling to God's promises and find your rest and security in him alone.

The Lord Is My Shepherd—I Have Life

Psalm 23:3 continues by saying that the Lord "restores my soul" or grants me life. Jesus picks up this language in John 10, where he says he is the Good Shepherd. Jesus gives rest and new life.

God brings those who are dead in their trespasses and sins and makes them alive together with Christ. The Good Shepherd rescues and gives life.

Labor and delivery is a good time to be reminded of what God has done through the cross of Christ. If labor is perfect, praise God. If labor has some special challenges, then praise God. He gives life together with Christ.

The Lord Is My Shepherd—I Receive Guidance

Psalm 23 reminds expectant parents that God offers them guidance. He offers this guidance in his Word (2 Timothy 3:16–17), and he offers it when his followers ask for wisdom (James 1:5). When you struggle with feeling like there is no guidance, Psalm 23 can reorient and encourage you.

Ten weeks prior to our first child's birth, we had moved in order for Rob to attend seminary. It was our first time living away from family and friends, in a town where we knew no one. Up until this point, I (Stephanie) had been working full-time as a nurse manager. After settling into our new home, Rob was working full-time and attending seminary, so my days seemed long as I awaited my next full-time job, motherhood.

Within a few days of his due date, our first baby was born. We did not know many people yet, but we had a few visitors. Although I was a little tired, my heart was still full of excitement and thanksgiving for the incredible privilege of being a mom, and I was thankful for the kindness of others who were willing to call or visit us. One particular lady, however, caught me by surprise. She noted how excited I was and then shared with me how I could expect to experience post-partum depression in the days ahead. She told me not to worry because it was common, and she had had it too. I can honestly say, that was the most interesting piece of advice I received.

But, this was not the first piece of advice I had received. Pregnant women seem to be magnets for ladies who want to share their thoughts, opinions, and wisdom on pregnancy, labor and delivery, and the early days of parenting. It happened to me, and I now witness it happening to others. I admit that not all the advice I received was bad; a fair share of it was based on personal opinions and experiences. But relying on the others' personal experiences as a guide for labor and delivery can easily lead to feeling fearful, anxious, and overwhelmed.

Dads, here is another connection point for you. We admit that dads are not offering as much advice as the ladies, but it still happens. Take the classes, visit the hospital, but remember that the book you will need in the hospital is the Bible and the truth it contains.

In the days leading up to your baby's birth, rely on God's guidance from his Word, because God's advice is advice that you are able to trust wholeheartedly.

The Lord Is My Shepherd—I Am Safe in Danger

Psalm 23:4 discusses those times when life is crashing. In the midst of danger or threats, God's rod and staff bring comfort. They are present when questions have no answers. God encourages his people so that they can follow the righteous path. His rod and his staff help his people to control their thoughts and fears.

This became a very real situation when our third child was born with the umbilical cord wrapped around her neck. It had not tightened until the final moments before birth, so the monitors did not catch it. However, as soon as the doctor saw it, he rapidly intervened. Rob was not given the opportunity to cut the cord this time because our child was in danger. In our case, our Great Shepherd allowed our little girl to be born without further complications. Even though she was in a very dangerous situation, our Shepherd decided to protect her from physical harm. As you know, that is not the case for everyone. Sometimes God allows tragedy in labor and delivery. Many of you know of someone who experienced a very difficult birth, or whose labor resulted in a permanent scar. We know that when the Lord allows these events to occur, he is also there to comfort, to give grace, to motivate his people to help, and to be with us each step of the way. We know that even if the Lord had not provided for our child as he did, our Shepherd would have led us through the valley of grief and hardship.

If God allows scary moments like a baby taken to intensive care, or mom rushed into emergency surgery, then remember that the Lord is your Shepherd. Please also reach out to family, friends, and your church for encouragement and support.

The Lord Is My Shepherd—I Have What I Need

The Lord gives security and provision. I encourage you to take notes and write down the ways in which the Lord has shown himself faithful during pregnancy. Considering the ways the Lord has already provided will allow you during labor and delivery to think on God's faithful provision. The past is a reminder that he is going to continue to be faithful in the moments ahead.

The Lord Is My Shepherd—I Have a Heavenly Home

This life cannot be lived solely for the here and now. The Lord expects his people to be good stewards of their opportunities here on earth, but believers are citizens of heaven (Philippians 3:20) and inhabitants of the holy city (Revelation 21—22). This future hope is a great reminder that there is always security.

New Fathers during Labor and Delivery

As we have already discussed, Psalm 23 is for dads too. In the labor and delivery room the attention is rightly focused on the mom and the unborn baby. But that does not mean that dad is out of the picture or irrelevant to the process. We dads still have the opportunity to pray with our wife, to serve her in ways that are appropriate at the moment, and to play gospel-centered music quietly so that our thoughts can be focused on the Lord. I (Rob) have some interesting stories you might find enjoyable.

You know that we have three children. It took three labors for me to figure out what I should be doing! While Stephanie was birthing our first child, I was very attentive. I held her, talked to her constantly, and caressed her arms and shoulders. Frankly, it was a bit overwhelming. I was even reading a monitor telling her when another contraction was coming, as if she needed to be told! But

I was a newbie. As a loving husband I wanted to do all I could to make the process as easy as possible. My heart was right, but the execution was lacking.

When Stephanie labored with our second child, I remembered my first experience and wanted it to be different. So I practically ignored her. I was so aware of not smothering her that I did not act much different than a picture on the wall. How is that possible? I went from one extreme to the other. That was my second new father fail. I wondered at the time whether there would be any possibility for redemption or whether I would have to live my life knowing that I had two opportunities to get my labor and delivery job right and failed both times.

Thankfully, we had a third child, which gave me the opportunity to avoid both extremes. I learned when I needed to give her a little space and when I needed to attend to her needs. I also learned to stop looking at the monitor to inform her that a contraction was coming. I still cannot believe I did that. (What kind of person does that?) We still laugh about my behavior and share it with others for their enjoyment. Not only can you take comfort in all the provisions the Lord has to offer, but also in the fact that you can always point back to me and tell your wife at least you are not married to that guy!

Praise God that Stephanie chose to forgive my failures and see that I was trying to love her—even if my love was very clumsy. I hope my experience encourages new fathers to see that God speaks to them about labor and delivery.

One Last Thought for New Moms

As new moms prepare for their own experience in labor and delivery, comparison and judgment are easy. Women have many choices to make for birth: natural or epidural, MD or midwife, hospital or home, bed or water. There are many different options from which to choose, and no option is more godly than another. The Lord will be your Shepherd regardless of the method you choose.

Exercises

1. Make a list of five significant ways that God has provided and cared for you during pregnancy.

2. Begin praying weekly for God's grace and strength through labor and delivery. Ask him to help you trust him as you prepare.

3. Attend the classes at the hospital and write out questions to ask at your next doctor's appointment.

4. Talk about how you believe Dad should act during labor and delivery. Attentive, aloof, somewhere in the middle? You can always change your plan if the situation warrants, but having an initial understanding of how Dad can be involved might be helpful.

Chapter 4

Be Prepared to Go Home

THE FIRST THREE chapters attempted to show that preparing for Christ-centered parenting has to do with several core truths. First, Christ must be our first love, must be the core of our identity, and must be the source of our strength and security. Second, God designed a married couple to work together. By the grace of God, we seek him both as individuals and as a couple, as well as trying to develop our relationship to the point that we are ready to welcome a child into our home. Third, a Jesus-centered approach to labor and delivery will help us rest and trust in the one who truly cares for us.

We thought there might be some benefit to addressing a few practical questions that arise prior to birth. These are likely not the only questions you have, but they pertain to some helpful matters to think through ahead of time: the "why" behind your equipment purchases, how to receive help from family and friends, and some practical advice about nursing.

First, the amount of equipment available to new parents is astonishing. It appears that people are willing to spend whatever is necessary to provide appropriate care for their child. Therefore, it is important to ask, *what equipment should I have when the baby comes home?*

Second, many women wonder, *what is it like to nurse a baby?* Stephanie will address the issue of nursing from the perspective of a Christian woman. This section is not a condemnation on those who choose not to nurse, but words of advice and encouragement for those who choose that method of feeding.

Third, as they bring a new baby into the family, many new parents ask, *What kind of help is appropriate?* They know the new baby is their responsibility, but Christian community can help as well.

Fourth, this chapter will explore how new parents can think biblically about the involvement of family in the early care of their baby. New parents may wonder, *What role should our extended families play in our child's life?*

Equipment

Solomon wisely reflected on his material possessions, saying, "Give me neither poverty nor riches; feed me with the food that is needful for me, *lest I be full and deny you and say,* 'Who is the Lord?' or lest I be poor and steal and profane the name of my God" (Proverbs 30:8–9, emphasis added).

We were the classic new parents who believed that every piece of equipment was necessary in order to make raising a child easier. Even though we did not have many funds to accomplish that task, we had very giving grandparents who were willing to help. As a result, we had a crib, a bassinet, a changing table, a car seat, a stroller, a Pack 'n Play, a special holder for diapers, a changing pad, a mobile for the top of the crib, a type of diaper trash can, and many other things that have long since disappeared. Additionally, we had diapers, wipes, toys, and clothes. Our nursery was absolutely amazing. Stephanie even did a Noah's ark stencil pattern around the room with a matching set of Noah's ark sheets, window valence, a toy, and a picture. Our nursery looked like a store designer decorated it. We were convinced that our child would not ever cry or be bored because his room was filled with so many things it would take years to study it all.

Since our children were born almost five years apart, we went through the baby, toddler, and pre-school stage three different times. After our second son was born, we did not believe that we would have any more children, so we gave away most of our baby stuff. Then, of course, our third child came along. Since we went through this stage three different times in three different homes, we found ourselves needing, and using, less and less. If only we had read Proverbs 30:8–9 when we had our first child.

We do not believe it is wrong to have a nursery with all the latest equipment for babies and a room with beauty from the ceiling to floor. There is a theology of beauty that follows the wonderful creativity of the Creator. But if you do not have such items, you are not failing as a parent. You can provide well for your children with very little.

Proverbs 30:8–9 describes two situations that are spiritually dangerous. In one case, people are so rich that they are able to look around and see that there is nothing more that they need. Such an attitude, according to the passage, can yield self-sufficiency and forgetfulness toward the Lord. These people stop praying, stop reading the Bible, and stop looking for Spirit-led answers. This attitude can easily tempt new parents. Be on guard.

In the other case, people are so destitute that they are continually tempted to steal because they are concerned that God will not provide so they take matters into their own hands. Such a place would be difficult for the parents and children. Thus, the author prays that God would give them an amount that allows them to rejoice at the success of others and yet remind them that they need the Lord to provide.

How do these two extremes help new parents prepare to bring home a child? First, new parents are dependent on the Lord for so many things with their baby. Many new parents are trying to be a good steward of God's gracious gifts. However, all parents have to remember that their child's life is always in the Lord's hands. Regardless of what beauty surrounds the child or what equipment makes it easier, parents always depend on the Lord.

Our extended family experienced the death of a young toddler. It was a visible reminder that life can be so delicate. Even before he died, there were many days of hurt, pain, and torment as his parents (and the physicians) tried to discover what was happening in his little body. Those months of unknowns were constant reminders that everyone needs the Lord's help.

Second, love for a child is expressed through more than equipment or room decor. Love is found through holding, caring, providing, and communicating. Material goods will not be the primary means of expressing love for little ones.

Third, each time we had a baby, we reduced the amount of equipment we had. Part of this came from learning through experience. Part of it was a growing conviction that the Scripture teaches us to provide for our children in ways that emphasize the Lord's provision.

The equipment that we suggest is our attempt to help new parents think about the things that might help them steward this opportunity well with a Proverbs 30:8–9 mind-set. We think it is pretty clear that you will have a crib, a car seat, and stroller. Those are virtually required. However, let us also say that two other things were well worth the money and served as a real blessing.

The most valuable piece of equipment, and the most unknown to us as new parents, was a breast pump. This one little device changed our lives and the number of tears that flowed in those early days. It gave Stephanie a little freedom in her day since she could pump and freeze some of her milk. The pump also made it easier for our children to nurse and prevented medical conditions like engorgement.

Second, we received a large Pack 'n Play. It allowed us to travel, to go to a friend's home, and gave us peace of mind that our baby was sleeping in a safe environment. In fact, this is one of very few items that we still own today. Many young couples have used it during events at our house.

Ultimately the choice of equipment is personal. You fill your nursery with whatever you believe will help you serve Jesus and your child well. Please also remember that love and care for the baby is not first expressed in the quality of their nursery. The baby is a gift from the Lord to you as people. Bought items will never remove dependency on the Lord, nor will they take the place of caring for children with love and grace. We believe that pleasing Jesus is not dependent on one's socioeconomic background, but on a heart seeking to honor Christ.

Nursing

Not every woman can nurse. Not every woman who can nurse chooses to nurse. We believe there is plenty of Christian liberty (Romans 14) for either option. Regardless of the option chosen, no one has to judge someone who walked another path. Those who have examined their life and come to the conclusion not to nurse are not going to hear judgment from us.

The Lord uses the nursing analogy to speak in general about care for others. Paul writes, "But we were gentle among you, like a nursing mother taking care of her own children. So, being affectionately desirous of you, we were ready to share with you not only the gospel of God but also our own selves, because you had become very dear to us" (1 Thessalonians 2:7–8).

This section addresses women who have chosen the path of nursing. How might nursing impact you, and how can the gospel shape those interactions?

Stephanie nursed each of our children for the first year of their lives. We chose this form of feeding for three reasons: Stephanie had a desire to nurse them, it was free, and it was convenient. It was also the analogy that Paul used to describe his ministry showing that nursing was a picture of Christlike care for another person.

For some, nursing seems very easy, yet for others, it can be very challenging. With our firstborn, nursing proved to be a little challenging due to our lack of prior knowledge and experience. However, it did not take long to learn, and nursing became even easier with each additional newborn.

Nursing for the first two weeks was uncomfortable for Stephanie until her breasts got used to it. We knew it took about three to five days after delivery to produce milk. What we did not know (at least experientially) was that when the milk comes, it is easy to become engorged. This simply means a woman may have too much milk. Because a new mom's breasts are hard and swollen, it is sometimes difficult for the baby to latch, possibly leaving both the mom and baby frustrated. One way to help with engorgement is by pumping each breast for a couple minutes prior to nursing. This allows just enough milk to be excreted in order for the breast to soften and make latching on more feasible.

Nursing was a blessing in many ways. I (Stephanie) remember looking down at my baby and seeing two beautiful little eyes looking back at me and feeling those precious little fingers wrapped around one of mine. That connection was a privilege. It was 1 Thessalonians 2:7–8 in action. I enjoyed the opportunity to bond with my children and care for them in this way. I also appreciated the convenience of nursing. Whenever they were hungry, warm milk was readily available and always at the right price. I am both humbled and fascinated to think about how God made my body to be able to care for our babies' needs right after their birth.

Nursing can also be a quiet time of encouragement for new moms. Once a little one enters the home, life gets busy. It is easy to push aside prayer and time in the Word. I encourage new moms to use one or two of their feeding times for these purposes. It will continue to help you focus on Christ even as you are serving the gift God gave you.

Appropriate Help

In Ephesians the metaphors for unity include one new man, one building, one body, and one household (see Ephesians 2:11–22). As a result, a baby born into a Christian home is also born into a community of people who care. Members of the Christian community have a special opportunity to bless new parents.

Parents who request help are doing the community a service. For example, when a new baby is born, the community has the opportunity to obey the Word of the Lord in providing help to those who need it. When people obey the Scripture, they receive satisfaction from knowing that they are living for Jesus.

When a community has the opportunity to serve, its members may develop a vested interest in the child. They may want to know if the child is growing; they may want to know what the child is doing; they may see victories in that family as community victories. This kind of community may be very different than our normal culture, but it is biblical. As others see the Christian community function, it can be a witnessing opportunity. We believe that new parents can be a blessing to their Christian community with requests for help when they keep the following in mind:

Serve the Community before the Delivery

Go to other people's showers. Make meals for them. Call those who are having a hard time in a particular area. When new parents have regularly participated in caring for others, then they are demonstrating that they are a part of the community.

The most obvious way to avoid taking advantage of the community is to be in it. Then giving the community opportunities to serve will be a mutual blessing. Those who are not part of the community by their actions may be much more likely to develop thoughts and behavior patterns of self-interest that take advantage of community kindness.

Request What Will Make a Difference

If people are going to serve one another, then they want the service to be meaningful. As parents of a new child, meals are a great request. Having meals for a week or two can make a significant difference. Help with food preparation may allow new parents to spend their time and energy on caring for their new child.

Other possible requests could be help with nursing or prayer.

Receiving Family

Newborn babies are like magnets. People love to see a new baby. We believe that the gospel message helps new parents with their response, regardless of the situation, including receiving family. As new parents consider the possibility of their parents or in-laws arriving for a period of time, we suggest they consider the following truths.

1. Hosting family is a privilege.

Some of you have wonderful parents. You cannot wait to share the joy of your new little one with them. Others of you have good parents and in-law parents, but they are far from perfect. Sometimes it is easy to complain about parents or in-laws. There might have been times when a parent or in-law did something that was not particularly helpful or encouraging. Maybe they were not as supportive of a decision as you would have liked. However, we encourage you to consider the possibility that having parents and in-laws who care and want to be involved is a privilege.

We understand that there are some situations where a parent or in-law should not be a welcome guest in the home. Some parents or stepparents have been abusive, and the safety of the next generation takes priority. What we are talking about here are times when it is tempting to shun one parent or another because they complain about how clean a closet is or make a rude comment about how their child is being cared for.

In many situations it would be a blessing and privilege to involve both sets of parents. If you are able to do that, then you should be thankful.

2. Hosting family is a chance to put Ephesians 6:2–3 into practice.

Paul writes, "'Honor your father and mother' (which is the first commandment with a promise), 'that it may go well with you and that you may live long in the land'" (Ephesians 6:2–3).

The original command, given in Exodus 20, was not meant solely for the young children in the audience. It was a command given to adults as well. God knew that mistreating one's parents would be a temptation for adult children. Thus, he codified in the Mosaic Law a concern for honoring parents as long as they live. This concern is also seen in the teaching of Jesus. Jesus rebuked the religious leaders for declaring their own possessions "Corban" and thus violating the command to honor parents (Mark 7:10–13). In their society the religious leaders created a little game. If you declared that your possessions were given to God (imagine this as a directive in your last will and testament), then you could still use them and they could not be given away. Jesus rebuked the leaders for this practice because it allowed the adult children to use all of their possessions, but would not allow them to share with their needy parents.

In our society we have to ask the question, How can I honor my parents? We encourage new parents to use the birth of a child as a special opportunity to bless and honor their parents. By allowing grandparents to come, to be involved with the baby, and to serve for a period of time, new parents are communicating to their parents and the Lord that they are seeking to obey God's Word.

In some cases, new parents may need to tactfully communicate that the stay will need to be limited to a certain period of time. However, we would still encourage new parents to find ways to honor their parents and allow them to be part of the joy of experiencing the new baby.

Exercises

1. Take one or two steps to ensure that you are actively engaging in the community.

2. Make a list of possessions that would be most helpful toward caring for your baby. We have given some ideas, but feel free to ask others as you create your list.

3. Review as a couple the key Bible passages that we have studied to this point in order to direct your thoughts as you prepare for parenting.

4. Discuss with each other how you might be able to involve your friends and family. What will you plan to ask your community (knowing it could change)? What could you ask your in-laws to do that would also be a blessing for them?

Chapter 5

Accomplish the Goal in Parenting

TO THIS POINT we have attempted to show that the gospel of Jesus Christ and the truths found in his Word form the foundation for believers' identity and relationship with him and their commitment to keeping their marriage relationship strong. Jesus, the Good Shepherd, comforts new parents' potential fears for labor and delivery, and he prepares them to bring home their new little gift.

We believe the next step in preparation to become a parent can be summarized by the question, what goal are we trying to accomplish? While there are lots of little goals along the way (for example, the goal to ensure the baby is eating), there is an overarching goal. There is a big-picture gospel goal that will form the foundation for all the other goals.

Parents must aim to glorify God by encouraging their children to love and worship the Lord above all else.

We believe it is helpful for you to have clearly in your minds what you are trying to accomplish. The clarity of a foundational goal keeps you grounded as you attempt to care for the little one in your home. There will be days that you feel like you are not doing it well. You may feel unsure of exactly what you should be doing.

Every parent—and we do not believe that is an exaggeration—has moments when they do not know what to do.

Remembering the Lord's goals for parents brings comfort and security. You know that you can repent and change when necessary and that grace is available for each day. Keep focused on honoring the Lord by his grace with your parenting.

Remember the words of Judges 2:10, "And all that generation also were gathered to their fathers. And there arose another generation after them who did not know the LORD or the work that he had done for Israel." You have the wonderful privilege and opportunity to participate in helping the next generation love and worship the Lord. We would like to look at this goal with three statements that define what it means to encourage children to love and worship the Lord.

Seek to Declare God's Praises

One of our favorite Bible passages regarding purpose or goal is 1 Peter 2:9–10. Peter writes, "But you are a chosen race, a royal priesthood, a holy nation, a people for his own possession, that you may proclaim the excellencies of him who called you out of darkness into his marvelous light. Once you were not a people, but now you are God's people; once you had not received mercy, but now you have received mercy."

Peter wrote to a group of people scattered across the known world who were suffering hardship. The hardship, however, is not what defined them. Believers in Christ have a clear and wonderful identity (remember chapter 1). Peter defines his audience's identity as a chosen race, royal priesthood, holy nation, and people for God's own possession. Please notice the purpose that flows from this identity—proclaiming the Lord's excellencies. The gospel message does not just change how we think about ourselves, but also how we seek to live. We proclaim or declare his excellencies (or praises) because of all that he has done for us.

Each of these descriptions in 1 Peter 2:9–10 has roots in Old Testament theology. The description "royal priesthood" is particularly applicable to new parents.

The priesthood was a special honor. A person had to be from the tribe of Levi and from the line of Aaron to be a priest. That person was to serve the Lord and his people. Rather than have their own land and their own means of generating income, the priests were servants of the Lord. Peter says that Christ's coming has changed the priesthood. Now, those who place their faith in Christ are priests but not just any kind of priest—royal ones.

While we were writing this book, there was a lot of excitement regarding the marriage of Prince Harry and Meghan Markle. News organizations often ran stories about the guest list, the invitations, and the events that would surround the wedding. I (Rob) admit that I found it a bit wearying. There were people in our church who were getting married, and CNN did not cover their ceremony. Two royal priests of the King of the universe were getting married and the news was not there to cover it. This may have found an outlet into a sermon.

Royal priests do not need the public's grand attention. Instead, they can focus on the joy of fulfilling their purpose—to proclaim the excellencies of him who called them into his marvelous light. King Jesus allows his children to declare his praises. Jesus gives his children the opportunity of telling others that they once lived in darkness and now live in the light.

New parents have the opportunity to live out 1 Peter 2:9–10 in a new way. The royal priesthood applies to believers before they become parents, but now, they have a new audience who needs to hear how God changes people through Christ. Children need to understand that having a new identity is possible. They need to hear early and often that a savior has come and he is able to give them a new and wonderful identity with real joy and purpose.

Dads, as you hold your new little one, you might say, "Honey, your mom and I are so happy that God gave you to us. We are so thankful for the opportunity that we have to hold you, to love you, to protect you, and to experience life with you. We want you to know that our God is a good God. He sent his Son to die on an awful cross to pay for my sins. When I was ten years old I understood that my sin was against the Lord . . ."

Or, "Honey, I was at work today and you would not believe what happened. God gave me the opportunity to help someone. A person came to me today and asked if they could talk. I learned that they were having trouble in their marriage. I told them what God has done for your mom and me. When I finished, I was able to encourage my coworker to seek help from our pastor. Isn't God amazing? I had no idea that was going to happen at work today."

Mom, you might say, "Sweetie, while you were taking a nap and giving Mommy a chance to rest, I was reading my Bible. Do you know what it said? God told me that I could pray to him whenever I was fearful and anxious. Sometimes mommy gets a little worried when you are not feeling well and God comforts us. Isn't he good?"

Telling children about the Lord does not only happen while parents are holding their babies. As children grow, there will be more and more opportunities to talk about the Lord. When parents talk about the goodness of God and about God's love and care, they are fulfilling their purpose to declare God's praises. God might use their testimony to open their children's eyes to their need to repent and trust Christ for their salvation.

2. Teach Your Child the Truths of Scripture

Moses writes to the Israelites and to new parents, saying,

> "And these words that I command you today shall be
> on your heart. You shall teach them diligently to your
> children, and shall talk of them when you sit in your
> house, and when you walk by the way, and when you
> lie down, and when you rise. You shall bind them as a
> sign on your hand, and they shall be as frontlets between
> your eyes. You shall write them on the doorposts of your
> house and on your gates.
>
> "And when the LORD your God brings you into the
> land that he swore to your fathers, to Abraham, to Isaac,
> and to Jacob, to give you—with great and good cities that
> you did not build, and houses full of all good things that
> you did not fill, and cisterns that you did not dig, and
> vineyards and olive trees that you did not plant—and
> when you eat and are full, then take care lest you forget
> the LORD, who brought you out of the land of Egypt,
> out of the house of slavery. It is the LORD your God you
> shall fear. Him you shall serve and by his name you shall
> swear. You shall not go after other gods, the gods of the
> peoples who are around you—for the LORD your God in
> your midst is a jealous God—lest the anger of the LORD
> your God be kindled against you, and he destroy you
> from off the face of the earth." (Deuteronomy 6:6–15)

God asks parents to teach their children the Bible. You can begin this process immediately, rather than waiting until children are older. How can parents teach their children God's Word? Deuteronomy 6:6–15 guides them.

First, the words of the Lord have to be on the parents' heart. People cannot teach what they do not know. New parents can seek help from godly leaders in their church. Parenting will push their understanding of Scripture sooner or later. Wise is the parent who decides to do some thinking in advance.

Here are a few questions that new parents face that require God's Word to answer:

1. How is God's character and goodness displayed in the Bible?
2. What does God tell me about my heart in the Bible?
3. What passages or concepts help me when I am discouraged or worried?
4. What passages teach that children should obey their parents?
5. What passages describe what biblical love looks like so that I can follow that pattern?
6. What passages help me to rejoice in my relationship with Christ?
7. What passages teach me about serving?

Second, parents can communicate God's words to their children every minute of every day (Deuteronomy 6:7–9). Children will learn from their parents, starting from the very first day. They learn what their parents value. They learn what their parents talk about and what excites their parents. Let these discussions seep with biblical love and wisdom.

Even though infants will not be able to respond to this teaching or understand all that you are saying, they know that you are talking to them. You, as parents, are establishing patterns of God-talk in their home. We encourage you to talk to your baby about the Lord. We believe the appropriate application of Deuteronomy 6 is not just a family Bible study, but a family that talks about and lives out the Bible to the glory of Christ.

New parents might have a conversation with their baby like the following:

> "You know, son, there are times when Dad and Mom have no idea what we are doing. We are new to this parenting thing. When we don't know what to do, we often think about Proverbs 3:5–6 which says, "Trust in the LORD with all your heart, and do not lean on your own understanding. In all your ways acknowledge him, and he will make straight your paths." There are going to be days when you don't know what to do. That is one reason we are praying for your relationship with the Lord. We want you to be able to lean on God so that he will direct your path."

Or something like this:

> "Sweetie, one of the easy things to do in life is complain. It seems to come to us. I know sometimes you are crying because you are telling us you need help. Maybe you need a diaper change or maybe your tummy hurts. We are so glad that you tell us because it helps us care for you. We also know that there are times that you cry and it seems like you just want to hear yourself talk. We understand that too. Sometimes after a hard day, I want to talk to your mom and I just talk and talk and talk. There are times when I come home, and Mom wants adult conversation with daddy. But there are other times, and this appears to be one of those times, that you are crying because you are complaining. I understand that too. But God's Word tells us that we are to do everything without complaining. We are not going to be perfect, but we need to work at learning to be thankful

for what we have and not to complain about what we do not have."

Use the everyday moments of life to teach the Word of God. We have a counseling ministry at our church that serves people from our congregation and our community. It is striking how little parents talk about the Lord. We encourage you to develop this pattern early. It will help you because you need to hear what you are saying to your children. It helps you because it establishes a normal pattern of God-talk in the home. While our very little ones will not fully understand or engage in these conversations until they are older, it is possible that they are still learning about our excitement for the Lord.

Third, materialistic care can sometimes deceive a person into believing that they do not need the Lord (Deuteronomy 6:10–12). Israel, for example, had been wandering in the wilderness for forty years. They gathered their manna on a daily basis. However, when they entered the land, they experienced a new reality. The land abundantly produced, and the nation gained material wealth that they did not work to achieve. When people do not rely on the Lord for daily provision, they might not rely on the Lord at all. Therefore, God, in his grace and goodness, warned his people that if they have what they want, their tendency will be to forget him.

New babies understand that they are dependent on others for care. New babies know that their parents provide for their needs. However, we believe it is important not to take too much credit. Parents must direct their praise to the Lord because their ability to provide is dependent on the Lord's grace.

It is wise to consider how a new parent might direct praise and worship to the Lord. Prayers before meals and before bed could remind children that God is the provider of all. Sharing Scripture, such as the story of Abraham, could begin to discipline parents and children to look for the God who provides.

For example, parents might say, "Daughter, God is an amazing provider. We were looking for a new children's ministry teacher for the second graders. We were almost to the point where we were going to combine classes because no one was willing to teach. Then, guess what? The Lord put it on Suzie's heart and she is going to teach. God knows exactly what we need when we need it. As you grow we are going to look for ways that God provides just like he provided that ram for Abraham in Genesis 22."

Fourth, when a person understands how wonderful and great God is, there is no reason to look for another god to worship. In our culture we do not worship statutes or erect temples to the names of gods like they did in biblical times. But the warning in Deuteronomy 6:13–15 can still apply to us. The nation thought that certain gods were real and offered value to those who worshipped them. The gods of Baal and Asherah were associated with fertility of land and people. Worshippers believed that these false gods could provide children and wealth. To say it another way, they believed that these gods would give them joy and satisfaction in their life.

We do not have these same kinds of idols in our society. However, as we mentioned earlier in this book, idolatry is placing anything as more important than the Lord. It is valuing something more than we value Christ. It is believing that joy, pleasure, and satisfaction come from something other than the Lord. Therefore, we can worship things that give us pleasure—sports, relationships, alcohol, work, or money. These are very real dangers in our world.

Starting from an early age, parents should teach their children that God does amazing things. God rescues people from their sins and delivers them from the power of sin. God provides for his children in amazing ways. God protects his children, even when they did not know they were being protected. God works in people's lives to help them see his greatness. The more parents talk about God's greatness, the more they are excited about it, and the more they build their lives around the worship of God, the less attractive idols will appear.

Let's take, for example, materialism. Our world will communicate to our children that they will be happy if they have an awesome home, car, wardrobe, phone, game system, and other goods—with money left over for trips to Disney. Parents can begin fighting against that idea in conversations like the following:

> "Yesterday we went to the Joneses' house. Their home is a blessing from the Lord. Always remember that material possessions are either used as a blessing from God or as a place of worship in our heart. The Joneses' shared their home with us today, and we were able to receive a blessing. We want you to use what God gives as a blessing to others as well. You have toys. We want you to use them for the glory of Christ by sharing. You will have a big bed someday. We want you to use it for the glory of Christ. Maybe you could allow a missionary to use it for a night. Remember, honey, material goods are either used to point people to the giver or cause us to focus on the gift."

New parents must dedicate themselves to teaching how wonderful God is. They must teach little ones how God does amazing things. New parents must teach that God is so much better and has so much more to offer than anything else. New parents must teach that no one loves them and their children like God.

3. Discipline Your Children without Provoking Them

Paul writes, "Fathers, do not provoke your children to anger, but bring them up in the discipline and instruction of the Lord" (Ephesians 6:4).

At some point in the near future, we recommend that you read chapter 2 of a book titled *The Heart of Anger* by Lou Priolo where he explains twenty-five ways that parents can provoke their children to anger. That chapter is easily worth the price of the book. It is especially helpful to read before you have angry children.

In short, Priolo states that parents provoke their children when they fail to create a home environment which protects them, provides for them, demonstrates love for them, and cares for them. Thus, parents who do not get along create a home that is unstable from the child's perspective. Parents who do not discuss the thoughts, motives, and feelings of their children do not care for them in each aspect of the Christian life. Parents who expect more from their children than they deliver themselves provoke them. This chapter assumes parents who are reading this book do not want to provoke their children, and that they are actively working toward not doing so.

Ephesians 6:4 still reminds parents, and fathers in particular, to bring up their children in discipline. This command includes discipline for an infant. Discipline, however, does not equal corporal punishment. Discipline involves rebuke and appropriate correction.

Parents can be committed to discipline even when their children are little. The discipline can look like a conversation. It is important, nevertheless. For example, by the time our children were a few months old, they were able to sit up and eat some solid food. Cheerios were a favorite. But it did not take long for them to realize that if they threw a Cheerio, it traveled a long way and the dog absolutely loved it. Is there discipline? Yes, but at first, the discipline is nothing more than telling babies no—and trying not to laugh as they giggle watching the dog chase the rolling Cheerio. At some point they understand, and when they do, it may be time to take away the Cheerios.

As babies grow, parents will have opportunities to talk about pulling hair, biting, or avoiding the stairs. The discipline is often little more than a conversation and maybe the loss of the opportunity for temptation. But these conversations form the foundation for a home to be gospel centered and not child centered. It sets the foundation for the continual focus on the truth of God's Word to be lived out in all the little moments of life.

We believe that when parents have a clear goal, they are much more prepared to handle the various changes and challenges that parenting bring. Parents never know what specific blessings or challenges a child might bring into their home, but they can know the target. Parents are going to do all they can from their very first day to help their little ones learn the gospel and understand that God's Word provides instruction and discipline that they desperately need.

Exercises

1. Restate the goal of parenting and then explain how that goal could help you as you parent. Think especially about parents you already know and how that goal either does or could help them in their task.

2. Pray with your spouse three times this week that God would help you adopt this goal and that you would remember it regularly.

3. Meet with another couple you respect who has children. Ask them how they declare God's goodness, teach their children, and use discipline. How have these helped them be intentional in their parenting? Ask them about one or two ways they failed to bring the gospel into a situation with their children.

Chapter 6

Work Together—
Not Against—
Each Other

CHAPTERS 2 AND 5 spoke about the importance of the marriage relationship and having a common goal in parenting. This chapter emphasizes another aspect—working together. God has called the parents to maintain their relationship as children are added to the home. This implies that parents work together. We know that there is a common goal, there is a common source of strength, and there is a common set of instructions. All too often, parents are divided about the child's care because there is a lack of humility, a lack of honest communication, and a lack of a dependence on Christ. This chapter will ask couples, in light of all that spouses share in common, to view each other as partners in the parenting process.

Need for Humility

James writes, "But he gives more grace. Therefore it says, 'God opposes the proud but gives grace to the humble'" (James 4:6).

We believe that caring for an infant is both a joy and a challenge. One of the greatest challenges is that infants cannot use language to communicate. Parents use language to explain their joys, hurts, challenges, wants, needs, and concerns. Infants cannot. As infants grow, there will be smiles, giggles, and looks of amazement. Sometimes, however, smiles are little more than gas. Giggles turn to frowns in milliseconds. Looks of amazement turn to fear. Many parents do not have any idea what inspired those looks or what to do about the changes in emotion. Such is the life of the new parent.

This phase of life is definitely not the time for pride.

Our first experience with a baby was our own newborn son. It was also Stephanie's first experience with nursing. Unlike feeding with a bottle, where the amount of intake is obvious, the quality of nursing is judged more by the output. Thankfully, a few days after our oldest son was born, her mother arrived for a visit. Having raised four children of her own, she could tell by looking at our son that he needed some nourishment. We did not realize that he was struggling with nursing. He was only about a week old, and we had not yet had our first doctor's visit. Stephanie's mom suggested a little bottle feeding, and our son drank like it was his last meal. In fact, there were a lot of things that happened that day.

Her advice came at just the right time. We thought our son was getting this sleeping thing down; it turned out he was lethargic. We thought he was nursing well; it turned out he was starving. We thought we knew at least some of what we were doing; it turned out we did not have any idea.

Within a week, our son was doing much better physically, and there was no sign of concern at his two-week appointment. We needed humility to listen to someone who could see what we could not see. Even though giving him a bottle would not make nursing easier, now was not the time for prideful bravado. Both of us needed to be willing to admit that we had no clue what we were doing, and we had to listen.

Consider the value of this scenario for young parents and a couple that had only been married for a few years. I (Rob) needed to be comfortable with the fact that Stephanie would call her mom for advice. This was not the time to accuse her of not leaving her parents or valuing her parents more than me. Yet, we have seen husbands criticize their wife for such actions.

At the same time, we have seen new moms react to their husbands in equally unhelpful ways. Imagine what would happen if a wife were to say to her husband, "My mom has raised children. How many have you raised?" Such a comment would be unloving and not gospel-centered. The comment would also be hurtful and prideful. Ephesians 4:29 explains that living worthy of the gospel involves communication that builds up rather than tears down.

Rather than responding with pride, it is best to humble yourselves and consider whether the Lord is graciously sending help in the form of a parent, friend, mentor, or doctor.

Humility in working together as parents also means being willing to listen to each other. There are times that husbands see things that wives cannot see. There are other times that wives see things husbands cannot see. Rather than having a spitting match about who is right and who is wrong, it is best for each person to listen carefully to the point being made by the other.

For example, if the wife decides to nurse, she will be up with the newborn. The husband may or may not be up, but she certainly will. Nighttime feedings can be tiring. A husband who sees his wife more tired than normal could encourage her to take a nap. It might mean missing out on time with her that day. However, by taking care of the baby while she sleeps for an uninterrupted hour, husbands will communicate love and appreciation to their wives.

Even today, now that our children are teenagers and adults, there remains the need to be humble. Teachers point out things we did not know. Coaches may be concerned about an attitude. Youth leaders may call to explain an issue. It is tempting to be defensive, to act like it must be someone else's fault, or to blame the concern on the person making it. Yet, the Lord may be using one of these servants to help you see something you are not seeing. Learning to be humble in the first days will help you recognize your need to be humble every day. Parents never figure it out. They rely on the grace of God that flows to the humble.

Need for Encouragement

Another way that new parents can work together is by encouraging one another. Paul writes, "Let no corrupting talk come out of your mouths, but only such as is good for building up, as fits the occasion, that it may give grace to those who hear." (Ephesians 4:29).

Ephesians 4:1 exhorts Christians to live in a way worthy of the gospel that they have received. One of the ways believers live consistent with the gospel is by encouraging one another. Ephesians 4:29 says that words should result in building up others. How might these passages apply to new parents?

New parents can sometimes feel very inadequate. They look at other parents and come to the conclusion that others are better. When wives are struggling, husbands could respond by saying, "Love, you are an amazing mom. We are all learning, but I see you loving and caring and doing the very best you can. Our baby is blessed by God to have a mom like you." When husbands are struggling, wives could respond by saying, "Thank you for getting up with the baby last night. I know you had to be at work today, and you must be exhausted. I want you to know that I and our baby appreciate you."

This model of affirmation also helps develop God-honoring patterns as children grow. Since Stephanie is a registered nurse, she has been the expert caretaker for all things medical. She knows when we need to go to the doctor and when a kiss and a bandage is the proper prescription. Rob, on the other hand, can panic about medical issues. As a result, Rob has had many opportunities to affirm the calm, controlled, decision-making process Stephanie follows in medical areas. Since one of our children is accident prone, there have been many opportunities for Rob to say, "Love, I am so thankful that you are so wise and thoughtful about medical issues. I am one blessed man and our children are blessed by a mom who knows how to care." At the same time, Rob was a better student, especially in math and science. This has given Stephanie the opportunity to encourage Rob as he helps with homework.

It is amazing what a little encouragement might do for the other. Sam Crabtree wrote a wonderful little book called *Practicing Affirmation* (Wheaton, Illinois: Crossway, 2011). It is a practical exposition of Ephesians 4:29. We encourage all couples to read it. If spouses are committed to encouraging one another, it will make their days much easier.

Encouragement can also occur at the level of actions. Paul writes, "So then, as we have opportunity, let us do good to everyone, and especially to those who are of the household of faith" (Galatians 6:10). Doing good is part of a gospel-centered life. It is worth considering ways that new parents can choose to do good to one another.

Appreciation can come in many forms. It could come in the form of a gift or a service provided. A husband could buy flowers for his wife. A wife could buy her husband a car wash gift card. Rob would not be the best gift giver in the world, but three times he got it reasonably right was shortly after the birth of each child. Rob bought a special gift for enduring labor and delivery. One time it was a bracelet, another time it was a necklace, and the final time it was a ring. These gifts were an opportunity to thank and encourage Stephanie. They also serve as potential keepsakes for the future. Stephanie could give the jewelry to the child whose birth prompted the gift. It could even be a special way to remember the gift of their mom after their parents are in heaven.

Other gestures of encouragement could be much simpler, like making coffee, packing a lunch, making dinner, taking someone to an appointment, or doing an extra chore around the house. The point is that new parents should be encouraging one another in both word and deed.

Need for Dependence

Solomon writes, "Trust in the LORD with all your heart, and do not lean on your own understanding. In all your ways acknowledge him, and he will make straight your paths" (Proverbs 3:5–6).

Infants cannot use language to communicate. While they communicate in other ways, the fact that they do not have language limits a parent's understanding. We did not know that our little one-week-old was hungry. We did not know that his lack of crying was at least partially due to becoming lethargic. These moments of uncertainty have not stopped. New parents can never know what God may allow into their lives. Christians can trust him in the midst of the unknown. Parenting can push believers to a greater dependence on the Lord because they are not in control. There will be new situations when you will feel unsure of what to do. As a couple, you can either acknowledge that this is the case, or you can pretend like you have it all together.

When our daughter was about three or four years old, she had a very serious allergic reaction. We did not know if she would survive. Within minutes, we were on our way to the hospital. By God's grace she was fine a couple hours later. However, to this day, we do not know what series of events set off that chain reaction of allergic chaos. We have a clear plan should that ever happen again. However, if it were our choice, we would prefer to know what caused the reaction so that we could avoid that poisonous combination. But we do not know. Instead, we have to trust the Lord.

One of our boys, when he was very little, decided that he did not want to brush his teeth. When we said that he needed to brush, he had a complete meltdown. He ran into his room and flopped himself on the floor and managed to split his head open as he slammed it into a little table. Where did that come from? This child was not particularly prone to these kinds of reactions. Yet, there we were in the hospital getting stitches.

Parenting is not formulaic. Parents are dependent on the Lord's help when their children are first born, but also as their children grow. The faster parents acknowledge their dependence, the better prepared they will be. When new parents agree that they need humility, encouragement, and dependence on the Lord, they will more easily work together.

Exercises

1. Create a list of ways you might be tempted to think you know more about child-rearing than your spouse. These are possible points of conflict in your future. Please ask the Lord to help you specifically develop humility in these areas.

2. Interview three couples: one who has raised their children, one who has older children (at least school age), and one who is in the early stages (has at least one infant). Ask them about some of the key lessons they have learned. Ask them what passages of Scripture helped them when they were unsure what to do.

3. Create a wish list of books from solid biblical authors whom you believe would help you as you start the parenting journey. We highly recommend *Shepherding a Child's Heart* (Tedd Tripp, Shepherd Press), *The Heart of Anger* (Lou Priolo, Grace and Truth Books), and *Age of Opportunity* (Paul Tripp, P & R Publishing).

Chapter 7

Stewardship of Sleep, Money, and the Heart

TO THIS POINT in the book, we have attempted to provide specific examples to help new parents think about real life with a newborn—their relationship with Lord and one another, the practicalities of labor and delivery, the need for community, and equipment to care well for the baby. With this foundation in place, what can those first few weeks of parenting look like?

We believe that children belong to God, just as everything belongs to God (Psalm 24:1). One implication is that parents are stewards of their children, just as they are also stewards of everything that God has given.

These stewardship responsibilities often compete with one another. Navigating these well requires wisdom. This chapter will discuss three areas of stewardship: sleep, money, and the heart. In our lives as parents and in our ministry to new parents, we see these three issues often dominate the first two months of life with a newborn.

Passages on Stewardship

Stewardship is an important topic in the Christian life. It is very different than the choice between right and wrong. Stewardship often involves the choice between what is good and what is excellent. It is often the difference between what can be done and what should be done. Consider the following truths:

- "Look carefully then how you walk, not as unwise but as wise, making the best use of the time, because the days are evil" (Ephesians 5:15–16).
- "So teach us to number our days that we may get a heart of wisdom" (Psalm 90:12).
- "And it is my prayer that your love may abound more and more, with knowledge and all discernment, so that you may approve what is excellent, and so be pure and blameless for the day of Christ, filled with the fruit of righteousness that comes through Jesus Christ, to the glory and praise of God" (Philippians 1:9–11).

These passages encourage Christians to balance their lives with the responsibilities that the Lord has given them. Balance involves making choices about the things that are excellent. It includes having the wisdom to know when it is time to sleep, to play, to save, to spend, to work, and to rest.

God has given each person different abilities, strengths, and weaknesses. That means each family might be a bit different. As long as parents are committed to stewardship, they will ask for God's grace to make gospel-centered choices.

Sleep and Baby Care

In our experience, there are few subjects that evoke stronger opinions and more animosity among brothers and sisters in Christ than whether it wise or helpful to attempt to schedule a baby's sleep and eating patterns. These patterns impact the ability of parents to rest. As a result they also impact stewardship of your life and your baby's life. We believe that these concerns can be needlessly divisive. Our advice is for new parents to do what they believe is best and not stand in judgment of those who choose differently (Romans 14). The Lord does not give direct instructions on how to handle an infant's sleeping and eating patterns. And yet, decisions about sleep are important choices for new parents. They can influence your work, your willingness to serve Christ in the little moments of your life, how you treat each other, and how you care for your child.

As you consider the upcoming birth, we encourage you to consider a few things. First, there is a significant difference between caring for a child who is physically and mentally healthy and one who is sick. Since I (Rob) grew up in a special needs family, my parents could not treat each of us the same. There were needs for my care and different needs for the care of my sibling. Some children struggle with health in a way that dictates how care will be given. Good stewardship demanded that my parents care for us in different ways. You will have to determine through God's grace what needs each of your children may have. Regardless of whether your child has many or fewer needs, you will have the special privilege of meeting them.

Second, guard against comparing yourself to other families. Parents may have good reasons to make choices that seem confusing to someone else. For example, some individuals work second or third shift. That means their day functions differently than those who work from eight in the morning to six in the evening. The decisions that you make regarding your sleep and feeding will be offered to the Lord in thanksgiving. We believe that a right understanding of Romans 14 allows parents to make decisions, offer those decisions to the Lord, and live free of feeling guilty because someone told them to do it differently. Those who make the decisions as a sacrifice of praise to the Lord and as a steward entrusted with a special gift from God can be assured that they are doing their best.

Third, you do not have to exercise stewardship the same way with each of your children. You are likely expecting a child for the first time. You might choose one way with your first child and realize that, for reasons known only to you, you believe you can honor Christ and be a better steward choosing a different path with a different child.

We are trying to make the point that being a steward of a little life is a tremendous privilege and responsibility.

As Stephanie and I were writing this book, we struggled with whether to say more. It would be easiest to move on and go to the next principle. But that is not how we do ministry in any other avenue. We are "out there" kind of people. We openly share our victories, our failures (who writes in a book that they ignored their wife during one of the births!), and our frustrations. We know firsthand that it is dangerous to be that open. It gives people the knowledge to hurt us or talk behind our back. We also know that the battle with our flesh remains. We know that our hearts are not always pure. But we take comfort in believing that what we share, we share for the good of others and the glory of God. Pay attention only to the parts where you see the glory of God shine bright, and reject those parts that are unhelpful. We share our story with a sense of fear and trepidation. We ask that you consider the reasons, the thoughtfulness of the actions, and then decide whether any of it is right for you.

When Stephanie was pregnant with our first child, we began to look at parents with infants differently. We were interested in what was happening in their life because we knew that we would soon be where they were. Was there a right way to steward this privilege? As we talked with others and searched the Scripture we could find no biblical reason why a schedule was godlier than no specific schedule (although many children will get on something of a normal schedule at some point). That led us to ask other questions like the following:

- Was a schedule better, worse, indifferent to our baby's health and development?
- How would the use of a schedule impact our marriage?
- How would a schedule impact our ability to worship on Sunday?
- How would a schedule impact our work outside the home?

These were stewardship questions in our minds. We decided that we would attempt to schedule our first child. We made that choice for the following four reasons:

1. We did not believe that a schedule was better or worse for a healthy child. Babies could thrive on demand feeding or with a schedule.
2. We believed that it was more likely that we could regularly worship if we had a rough idea of when our child would eat, sleep, and play.
3. We believed that growing our relationship as a couple would include times of caring for the baby together and times of being alone.
4. We believed that we would be able to handle our work and educational responsibilities best if we had a regular time to rest.

It is also important to remember that parents seek the counsel and wisdom of their pediatrician. There are times when schedules, for those who want them, have to be modified for the health of a child. There are even times when those who do not schedule are advised to schedule in order to ensure the baby has sufficient nourishment. Earlier we mentioned that our child needed supplements for a period of time. Thus, we encourage parents to think wisely, follow the counsel of their physicians, and do their best to honor the Lord while serving their child well.[4]

We learned a few things about scheduling that might save parents who follow that method a little heartache.

- Our schedule was a guide. It was not "Thus says the Lord." The times changed on certain days, and not every child progressed at the same rate.
- Whenever we changed times, there was a three-day adjustment period. We all have normal times when we eat and sleep. When those are interrupted (for a trip to another time zone, for example) there is often an adjustment period. That is true for a child as well.
- The first several weeks were especially difficult because it seemed like one long day with neither a daytime or a nighttime. But once we made it to the point where our child would sleep five or six hours at night, it changed life.

Again, we want to say that there are many reasons why a schedule might not be the best option. It is not the only way to please the Lord. A schedule was an application of stewardship principles that served us well, and our pediatrician did not discourage our plans.

Whatever ways that families attempt to steward their lives, we believe that there are many gospel moments. There will be crying. Will you rely on God's grace and comfort to also comfort your child? There will be moments of frustration. Will you steward them well, looking for how God might want to grow you in this frustrating moment? There will be moments of bliss. There will be

---

4. For those who are curious, we started out with feedings every three hours around the clock. Once we had to wake up our child on a regular basis, we moved to every three and a half hours. As the child grew we could move to every four hours. By the time our child was old enough for some solid food, they ate when we did. If you want more specifics, please speak to your mentor.

moments of confusion. There will be moments of joy. It will all be there. Living out the gospel will require that new parents respond in a God-honoring way to these moments.

Money and Lifestyle

As you consider how your budget and lifestyle will change with a child, we encourage you to talk regularly to one another and pray that the Lord would grant you wisdom. Certain aspects of life may change, but change is not always bad. In fact, change may be very good, especially if new parents respond in a Christ-pleasing way.

One area you will have to consider is whether either Mom or Dad will choose to stay home full-time with the baby. In our ministry, we encourage couples to think about their finances both prior to and after having children. We emphasize flexibility and not creating financial burdens that require two incomes. If couples have developed a lifestyle that is supported on one income, then they are able to decide whether they want one parent to stay home with a child. We do not believe that God commands that one parent stay at home. Instead we believe it is wise for people to make it possible to have that choice. Whether they choose to exercise it or not is a personal and family matter.

We were a two-income, no-kids family before our first son was born. However, we chose not to create a lifestyle based on what we earned. We believed that we could control our spending—with Christ's help. We chose to live on Rob's income. Stephanie's income was only used for projects. It could be a special savings, giving, or purchasing opportunity, but it was always a one-time thing. When we lost her income, the adjustment was simple. We cut out the special projects.

Couples who choose for both parents to work after their Family Medical Leave Act (FMLA) expires should also recognize that things will change. They will have to pay for day care. If Mom chooses to nurse, then she will have to pump at work. Someone will need to drop off and pick up the child at day care. When the baby has a rough evening, it can be a very challenging experience for everyone. Our encouragement is to think about the implications of both options and ask the Lord what he wants.

Stewardship has a lot of different components. Those components often compete. Money, time, lifestyle, caring for children, and the like must all fit in the same twenty-four-hour day. Since you cannot adjust the time you have, you must make stewardship choices about how that time will be spent.

The Heart

The final area that we would like to discuss related to stewardship is of a parent's own heart. Solomon encouraged, "Keep your heart with all vigilance, for from it flow the springs of life" (Proverbs 4:23).

New parents must be careful to worship Christ, not their schedule, work, or one another. There is only one worthy of worship. We encourage you to remember that all of the options have their own implications. Following Scripture and setting your affections on Christ results in stewardship that looks different from home to home.

How do new parents steward their hearts as they make decisions about childcare and employment? These choices can be filled with anger, jealousy, regret, bitterness, and more. Instead, they can trust in the Lord and ask for his grace each step of the way.

What can new parents do about time flexibility? One reason we scheduled our babies' feeding and sleeping times was to have a more predictable approach to life. Even then, sometimes the best laid plans did not always work. We did the best we could, knowing that the Lord provides mercy and grace to help in our time of need (Hebrews 4:14–16). We knew for sure that we needed to steward the attitude of our own hearts.

What about stewarding the heart when it comes to expenses? Children cost money. We do not write that with a complaining spirit. It is just a fact. If families change their work schedule and add expenses, then the budget gets pinched on both sides. Finances are always for the Lord. You may have to think more carefully about the present and the long-term. This has an application to your hearts as well.

Exercises

1. Create a preliminary plan for after your baby is born. Include in your plan feeding/sleeping schedules, work schedules, and your new estimated budget.

2. Interview two couples—one who used a schedule and one who did not. What experience did they have? If they had another child, would they stay with the same option or change? Why? This could add perspective to your choice that would help you better understand the implications of your decision.

3. Pray that God would help you steward your life and the life of your little one for his honor and glory. Ask him to give you wisdom in the moment and to help you remember his Word.

Chapter 8
The Blessings
of Parenting

WE HAVE TRIED to describe how Christ makes a difference in how couples work together, what purposes and goals they work toward, how they think about family and the nursery, as well as stewardship related to the early stages of a child's life. We endeavored to be open, honest, and realistic about welcoming a first baby into the home. Honest talk, however, can give some the impression that infancy is a stage to survive rather than thrive.

We believe that parents who are properly focused on Christ can enjoy every stage of their child's development. Each stage has its own set of blessings and challenges, but gospel-focused parents are thankful parents. Think with us about three simple truths describing every child.

Every child is an image bearer of God. Every human being is a visible representative of the God who cannot be seen. Expectant parents are about to be given one of the most wonderful responsibilities that a person could ever have. Parents have the opportunity to care for, love, cherish, and raise an image bearer of the Creator.

The Lord himself crafted every child (Psalm 139:13–16). That makes every child precious in the sight of God and in the sight of his or her parents. With modern technology, expectant parents can see the developmental process in the womb. They even have the opportunity to have pictures of their little child and to post those pictures on their favorite social media sites. While new parents marvel at the various stages of development, they must also remember that God is weaving their baby inside Mom's womb.

God gives every child gifts and abilities. Rob, for example, had a desire for competition and athletics, but God did not give him the athletic ability. Two of Rob's uncles earned Division I scholarships for their athletic accomplishments, but there were other gifts that God gave Rob. Parents can celebrate the gifts and abilities God has given each child.

These basic gospel truths set the stage to help parents enjoy their child's development. Parents can enjoy the stage their child is in and anticipate what God will do with the child in the next stage. We have outlined the blessings we experienced as parents in each stage. A book like this cannot possibly discuss all the little blessings. Instead, these are some categories. We encourage you to keep a mental (or maybe physical) list each day of the blessings associated with caring for a child during different stages.

Blessings of Infancy

Infancy will be the only time in their lives that a child's whole body will fit on a parent's chest. Both of us remember the days when our infants would fall asleep with their little head under our chin and their entire body barely reaching our lap. We wanted our children to learn to sleep on their own. However, there were plenty of times we held them until they fell asleep because we loved it. That stage only lasted a short time, and it was a stage to which they never returned. In fact, as our children grew physically, we would often tell them that they were growing too fast. Enjoy every single one of those snuggle times. Thank the Lord for the gift of life and the gift of this little one.

Infants change rapidly so every day seems like a new adventure. One day newborns may seem oblivious to their parents, and the next day they smile. Then their clothes do not fit, and the next day they make a sound that must be a word. Soon, infants are turning over, and crawling follows shortly thereafter. Rob would come home from work and inevitably there would be a story about something that our baby did for the first time. Of course, as soon as something new happens, parents want their infants to reproduce it. For example, one of our children turned in their crib. We were so excited. We laid this child in the crib and stood there waiting for it to happen again. Those were great times. We loved wondering what the new day would bring. Change was rapid, and change was a chance to give thanks to the Lord.

Infants also need their parents in a special, sweet way. The days of independence are coming. There will be a day when your child will want to use the car. There will be a day when they want to spend time with their friends, and a day when friends have a prominent influence. But in infancy, parents are primary. Little ones need help getting dressed, changing clothes, taking a bath, finding food, and getting out of bed. What a blessing to care for another human being in these ways. When their baby needs help, parents can thank the Lord that they had the opportunity to provide it.

Blessings of Toddlers

Toddlers are incredibly creative and have wonderful problem-solving abilities. One of our toddlers talked one of the grandmas into playing a game of hide-and-seek. He then locked her in the closet and left. Thankfully, it did not take long for us to let her out. We realize that there were some discipline opportunities there, but we marveled at his creativity. Where did he come up with that one? We were seeing different aspects of being made in the image of God on display before our eyes. One of the great blessings of toddlers is watching their minds work.

Toddlers are also learning language and making mistakes along the way. It is so cute to hear a two-year-old speak. Each of our children had a word or phrase that sounded precious but was entirely wrong. One child told us he needed to put his "glubs" on. A different child wanted some "m&m&ms." It is even more wonderful to hear Mom interpret.

Rob greets at the front door of the church every Sunday. As families walk by, occasionally a two-year-old must explain something. I have no idea what they are telling me. But I know they know, and I know Mom knows. A little glance her way, and she interprets. Again, this is a stage that passes quickly—so enjoy it.

I (Rob) remember when one of our sons and I were going to have a tent night. He was about four years old. By now everyone could understand his language, but there were still wonderful language moments. Tent nights were times when one of the boys and I would set up a tent in the living room, watch a movie, and eat junk food. One particular tent night I said something to which our son responded "shut up." Caught a bit off guard, I asked, "What did you say?" He responded, "I said, 'shut up.'" I was still trying to process this series of events and asked again, "What?" He said, "I SAID, 'SHUT . . . UP!'" In that moment, it hit me. I started laughing uncontrollably. I suddenly realized that our little toddler had seen a TV commercial where the phrase "shut up" was used to mean "no way—that is amazing." At first, I thought he was being disrespectful, and what I realized is that he was saying "no way—that is amazing." Those little language errors can make the toddler stage very enjoyable.

The toddler stage may provide many opportunities to share the gospel. Toddlers start to become aware of their own wills and their own desires. They want to exercise those desires. When they do, it provides a great opportunity to share what each child needs to hear about Jesus Christ's death, burial, resurrection, and return. Parents cannot force their child into a profession of faith. The Spirit needs to awaken individuals; however, parents are responsible to share the message of Christ. The toddler years provide great opportunities.

Toddlers provide opportunities for parents to check their motives as well. It can be hard to know what a toddler understands, until they understand. We remember telling one of our boys to be careful around electrical outlets. He seemed fascinated by them. His fascination only intensified when he learned that caution was needed. We can still picture the day our son was looking at us and holding his finger inches from the outlet. It seemed like he was saying, "I am going to touch the outlet. What will you do about it?" In that moment, parents can learn about their own motives. Is that moment about the parent's pride, or is that moment about Christ?

Blessings of Older Children

We are going to define "older" as school age. Older children communicate with language. We loved being able to speak with our children and enjoy mutual understanding as one aspect of our relationship. Older children may be able to express their love in more tangible ways. They give big hugs and slobbery kisses (these come in the toddler stage as well). They color pictures and make little crafts. Rob has many assorted candy dishes that were gifts in this stage. We enjoyed the closeness that we developed as a result of their expressions of love.

Older children can also be surprised. It is fun to surprise them. One year we decided to take our children to Disney World in Florida. For months we counted down the days. They were so excited. They knew that we were leaving on a Saturday. Our youngest was four or five. In God's sovereignty our big surprise was that the airline decided to change our flights. We made a few special arrangements, and we were going to leave a day earlier instead. But we did not tell them. To see the expressions on their faces when they figured out what was happening was priceless. Surprising our children with that extra day at Disney was a blessing from the Lord and one of our favorite memories.

It is often fun to see older children understand more about faith. We believe that talking to children about Jesus can start early—even in the womb. Older children can relate the truth of Scripture to the events of their lives.

Enjoying the Blessings and Limitations

We briefly mentioned this topic in the second chapter. However, we believe it deserves a longer treatment here. Some parents have the joy of welcoming a child with physical or mental challenges into their home. Earlier we mentioned that every child has a series of gifts and abilities from the Lord. Each one is a special blessing. Every child also has certain limitations. Some of the limitations are physical, others intellectual, and others emotional. Parents have the opportunity to provide special care in the way each child needs care.

In the sovereignty of God, none of our children were physically ill. They struggled with the standard reflux, an occasional cold, croup, and things of that sort, but we do not have children with significant physical or mental disabilities. However, both of us grew up in homes with siblings with various kinds of physical or learning challenges, and we have ministered to those whose children were not as healthy as others. We believe it is wise to prepare you with a few ideas should the Lord give you a child with a different set of blessings and limitations than you were expecting.

First, remember the theological truths this chapter outlined about all children. If every child is made in the image of God, then every child is special to God. People who have disabilities have very special aspects of their character, personality, and function.

We watched our own parents and other parents speak of the joy that each child brought into their life and the unique ways that they contributed to the family. Parents will see those things better than anyone else.

Second, seek to help children with their limitations rather than unnecessarily limiting their future. Even if a child has significant difficulties and limitations, that does not mean God cannot do something amazing. Joni Eareckson Tada is an example. After a diving accident left her paralyzed, Joni has managed to rally many resources for the disabled community for God's glory. Each child has a gift and limitation package. Encourage the gifts and provide help in the limitations. God has a wonderful plan.

Third, rely on the Lord as your greatest source of strength as you learn to care for your child. Their limitations might not allow certain kinds of care and they might demand other kinds. Lean into the Lord (James 4) with humble dependence knowing that grace flows in your direction. The limitations will have certain consequences, but they may also provide a means to grow closer to the Lord.

Fourth, celebrate, appreciate, and give thanks for the child's qualities that are special. Rob's sister was born with spina bifida, a condition that comes with varying degrees of physical and mental limitations. She was able to process mentally as if there was no birth defect, but her physical condition was very different. She had a wonderful sense of humor. She could come up with some of the funniest comments. It was part of her blessings package. It was part of what made her unique. Parents (and families) who learn to celebrate the gifts of their children will enjoy and appreciate this opportunity.

One young couple we know longed for a child, and after a couple of disappointments, they finally celebrated their first child's birth. It did not take long to learn that their baby struggled in ways that other newborns did not struggle. As the weeks and months went by, this couple learned that there were some things about their child that were going to be different than those of other children. It was easy to allow jealousy and heartache to enter, especially when they were tired or when they learned that another baby was doing something that theirs could not. This idea of a gifts and limitations package helped them. They saw their child as a wonderful gift made in a very special way to bring glory and honor to God. They saw the limitations of their child as an opportunity to show genuine love to their baby. The more they embrace who their child is and the special package that God gave their child, the more their hearts rejoice at the blessings of parenting.

We believe this chapter belonged in this book because there are unknown and potentially scary things about pregnancy, labor, delivery, and raising an infant. However, there are also many joys. Enjoy learning to trust God more. Enjoy learning about one's own limitations. Enjoy the many blessings that each stage of life brings. Enjoy the gifts package that God gave, and provide help and encouragement regarding whatever limitations your child may have. This is such an exciting time in your life, and we hope you have great joy in the Lord in the midst of it.

Exercises

1. Ask the Lord to help you always value this little gift and to see their gifts and limitations as tailor-made for bringing glory to their Creator.

2. Ask the Lord to help you develop the habit of speaking about your child's gifts and abilities from an early age.

3. Ask a couple friends in your church about the different stages of their child's development. What did they enjoy most? Why?

Chapter 9

Dad's Involvement

WE BELIEVE THAT fathers have a very important role in parenting. The Scripture says, "Fathers, do not provoke your children to anger, but bring them up in the discipline and instruction of the Lord" (Ephesians 6:4).

We know that some commentators believe that the word *fathers* here refers to parents. The argument is that the word for parents is used earlier in Ephesians 6 and the author chose a different word in verse 4 for stylistic reasons. We are not convinced. We believe that the purpose for the change in terminology was to highlight the particular role that a father is to have in the life of his children.

Our interpretation does not minimize the role of a mother. In fact, the book of Proverbs includes many speeches that begin with the words *my son*. These "my son speeches" are often started with a call to listen to the instruction of a mother and a father (for example, Proverbs 1:8; 6:20). Thus, the Bible is not calling out fathers in Ephesians 6:4 to the exclusion of the mother. Instead, it is addressing men in particular. It is quite possible that some of the same mind-sets one finds in today's culture are similar to the mind-sets of other cultures; namely, the temptation men face to leave the responsibilities of raising children to their mothers.

Some of this temptation is rooted in culture where men view themselves as providers for the home and women view themselves as caretakers. Admittedly, American culture today differs from what it was in 1950, but in our counseling ministry today, we often find it more difficult to talk to Dad about his parenting than Mom about hers. Why? Dads may believe that their contribution (normally having something to do with provision) has been fulfilled and the behavior issues associated with the children are the mom's problem. So although many women work outside the home and contribute to the family in various ways, woman are often still expected to carry the load of child-rearing.

We believe the Bible speaks directly to fathers and exhorts them to be actively involved by taking responsibility for their children. It is possible for dad to bond with a baby, to care for a baby, and to be involved in the decision process at each stage.

The Bible describes the role of fathers using a series of commands. The first command in Ephesians 6:4 is "do not provoke your children to anger." In his book, *The Heart of Anger*, Lou Priolo lists twenty-five ways that fathers provoke their children to anger. It is one of the most significant chapters on parenting ever written. Priolo contends that most of the twenty-five ways that fathers provoke their children have their roots in poor relationships with Mom or with the children. (These relational problems also have roots in their relationship with Christ.) For example, children are more inclined to anger when Dad does not treat Mom with kindness and love. Without a culture of love and kindness between the parents, a child's world is insecure and unpredictable.

Earlier chapters in this book emphasized the relationship between husbands and their spouses. This chapter emphasizes the relationships that dads develop with their children. We believe that many poor relationships between father and child begin with a pattern that starts shortly after birth. Dads convince themselves that their role is not very important in the early days and follow that pattern as the days pass. We believe that fathers who want to take this command seriously will seek to establish a healthy and strong relationship with their children from their birth.

Instead of provoking children, Ephesians 6:4 tells fathers to bring them up in the discipline and instruction of the Lord. These commands, one given negatively (do not provoke to anger) and the other positively (bring them up) play a significant role in how the father will be engaged in the parenting process. It is important to remember that Ephesians 6:4 still carries the command of Ephesians 4:1 where Paul says to live in a manner worthy of the calling to which believers have been called. In other words, gospel-centered living for fathers involves not provoking and bringing up their children.

How does it look to live out this verse when a child is still a baby?

Celebrations

Dads should be involved in celebrating new things. Babies do new things regularly. They smile; they giggle; they turn over; they somehow manage to move into awkward positions; they show excitement; and they show various other emotions. Sometimes it is easy to ignore these moments or to see these moments as routine or unimportant. But what if dads were able to see those moments as opportunities to praise the Creator who made their children and designed them? What if that smile were seen as the wonderful plan of God in motion?

Rob can remember coming home from work many times and finding out that a child did something new. At times, it was not all that exciting. After all, he had a seminary paper to write; work to do; lawn to cut; and plans to organize. Besides, there were times (like turning over) when Rob would go to the child, encourage him to turn for Daddy just like he did for Mommy, and stand there to see it happen. He would watch and watch and watch. Eventually he would stop watching, lose the moment of celebration, and do something else.

All too often moments like this become the normal pattern for life. The child does something new and Dad does not really care. Much better is celebrating what the child did and rejoicing over God's blessings.

Household Duties

Dads should be involved in household duties. If you read *Tying the Knot*, then you know that we encouraged engaged couples to perform their God-given roles. Husbands, for example, are to love, learn, and lead. These are nonnegotiable. However, there is also the way that a couple does life. How they handle the shopping, the cleaning, the laundry, the finances, the cooking, and all the other duties are open for learning and adjusting. The process of learning and adjusting is a journey. Many husbands and wives have found a great balance so that both husband and wife have meaningful and productive responsibilities at home.

However, we use the word *journey* for a reason. As life circumstances change, these household duties have to be revisited. Fathers should check to be sure that what was sustainable before the baby is sustainable after the baby.

Dad can consider and monitor how the birth of a child changes the responsibility chart. Some women will move from the workforce to being at home. In that case, a wife may actually take more of the household duties. Some will have time off and then return to work. Two different situations might require two different divisions of labor. Wise is the new father who considers what changes should be made in light of new and changing circumstances. Wise is the new father who sees this as part of his involvement in fulfilling his Christ-centered privilege in the home.

Childcare

Dads should also be involved in feeding, changing, and playing. I (Rob) remember when our firstborn came home. In our case, Stephanie was not planning to work outside the home, while I had a job and was going to graduate school. That meant that Stephanie did a lot of the care because she was more available than I was. In addition, since Stephanie nursed, it often seemed to me that I was of little value. It was not that I wanted to ignore my duties, but it seemed like I was an unnecessary part of the process. That was wrong thinking. Thankfully, God gave me additional opportunities at the baby stage to handle matters differently. What I later learned was the joy and fun of being involved in these moments as well.

We want to encourage new dads to participate. If Mom is nursing, then Mom will normally (close to always) be part of the routine for baby care. However, there are other duties to perform. Babies still need to be changed. Playtime is also a part of caring for babies. Holding your child, talking to them, and loving them are also important baby duties. Dad, you can, and should, be part of that process.

Dads who are actively involved in the care of their children are not just providing some relief to Mom by supervising playtime or changing the baby. Sometimes we hear dads speak as if they need to babysit their own children. Dads do not babysit; they parent. Allowing Mom to rest while dad takes care of the child is a worthy objective, but the primary focus is not giving mom a break. Dads who view baby care as serving their wives may still view the mom as the primary person responsible for parenting. This mind-set runs counter to gospel-centered parenting.

The focus is for dad to be involved in caring for the well-being of the baby. By caring for the child directly, Dad is actively applying Ephesians 6:4 and setting a foundation of taking responsibility for child-rearing.

Instruction and Discipline

The positive command in Ephesians 6:4 is to bring up the child in instruction and discipline. In order to be a Christ-centered parent, fathers must take responsibility for instruction and discipline. Instruction has many different forms and so does discipline.

Instruction could involve explaining something, showing how to do something, doing an activity together, or providing guidance while someone else does something. Discipline also has many different forms. Some Christians may equate discipline with corporal punishment, but we do not. We believe discipline can range from having a conversation to removing a privilege to assigning a consequence—and every step in between.

How might Dad be involved in instruction?

One example might be helping a baby learn to fall sleep on their own. You might choose to hold your baby or rock your baby to sleep on some occasions, but there are other times that is difficult to do. Let's pretend it is time for bed and you have provided all the proper care—your child has a full tummy, clean clothes, a comfortable environment, and a safe place to sleep. But your child decides they would rather not fall asleep on their own and instead begins to cry.

It is unwise to let a child cry unattended. Circumstances may change and there may be a good reason why the baby is crying. One of our children managed to wedge his leg between the bars of the crib and he could not move. We have no idea how he did that, but he needed help and comfort. Other times, they needed a clean diaper or did not feel well and needed to be comforted. But other times it was an opportunity for instruction. Instruction and training might be as simple as holding your child, hugging them, reminding them that they need to go to sleep, and laying them back down. If the crying continues, parents may need to consider whether other issues are occurring. Parents want to train, but also properly care.

Our point is that one possible opportunity for early instruction is learning to go to sleep, and Dad has to be involved in that process.

Discipline begins later. We do not focus on discipline at the infant stage, but one of the early opportunities for discipline is mealtime. As children grow, their desires are expressed in many ways. Mealtime often means that things are hot. A pan of hot water or a hot burner is dangerous. Food is a wonderful thing to toss across the room, or to give to the dog, or to put all over your body. Too often it is Mom who has to handle this. This sets in motion a family culture that fails to fulfill the worthy gospel living found in Scripture. These early discipline issues do not always seem important, but they set the stage for how Mom and Dad will function in the later toddler years when high-handed defiance, back talk, and expressions of sinful anger become more common.

Sometimes, new fathers do not see instruction and discipline as an important part of their duty in these early years. However, the more dads are involved in owning these responsibilities from early childhood, the more they will live out the gospel in their homes. An added benefit is that their wife will not believe that she is responsible for all the parenting.

Decisions

Dads should also be involved in decisions. There are many decisions that occur with a baby. New parents have to decide whether they will schedule or attempt to schedule a newborn's feeding and sleeping. If new parents schedule, then they will have to decide how closely they want to keep that schedule. New parents have to decide when they will take the baby to church and how they will handle nursery. They have to decide how involved they will stay in their small group. They have to decide if they will continue their regular dates, and, if so, who they will allow to care for their infant. They have to decide when to take the child out in public and when it would be best to remain indoors. They have to decide who their pediatrician will be.

There are many decisions that have to be made, and each decision should have Dad's involvement. We do not believe that dads have to make all the decisions. However, if Dad does not actively engage in decisions, then he may not feel like he is a part of the parenting process. At the same time, his wife may feel very overwhelmed if all these choices are hers.

I (Rob) had to learn this lesson as well. When our first child was born, I had a lot going on in my life. I often wondered if I had taken on more responsibility than I could manage. In addition, I am generally laid back. Some things do not bother me one way or the other. For example, I often did not have an opinion about whether our baby needed to go to the doctor, whether our plans and schedules for the child were appropriate, or whether we should go to a particular event. I thought I was being flexible. I thought I was making it easy. However, I was not willing to see that my casual attitude toward a lot of life decisions placed a lot of pressure on Stephanie. What I thought was making it easy, was in fact, making it hard. My carefree attitude about life decisions made it seem like I cared very little about her and her life.

What I had to realize is that I was not walking worthy of the gospel because I was too busy walking worthy of my idols (finishing education and working). I needed to care about these choices because that is what Ephesians 6:4 calls fathers to do. Then I needed to support those decisions by helping to implement them.

When Baby Wants Mom

One of the obstacles dads have to overcome in parenting is the big picture cultural mind-set that child-rearing is Mom's responsibility. But there is another—when baby wants Mom.

Imagine it is nine in the evening. Dad arrived home at six in the evening after a day at work. He worked hard, did his best, and then came home and helped with a few duties around the house. It is almost bedtime, and Dad knows with certainty that he will be up at some point during the night. Mom fell asleep on the couch, and the baby is crying. The baby does not need fed or changed so Dad decides to hold the baby because he wants to serve his wife and care for his child. Here is a golden opportunity for some snuggle time with the little one. The problem is that this little bundle of joy will not settle down. Dad sits and rocks, but his efforts do not work. He stands and lightly sways, but his efforts do not work. Dad plays some soothing music and sits and stands, but his efforts do not work. Mom hears the baby and walks in the room. She politely says, "Thanks for caring for us, Babe. Would you mind if I try?" As soon as the baby is in her arms, the crying stops. Dad cannot believe it.

Dads often know in their heads that their baby spent nine months inside of their wife's womb. Babies hear Mom's heartbeat for nine months and experience protection and security inside her. Even though dads know those things, the reality that it is easier for the baby's mom to calm the child still hurts the heart. Dads may be tempted to be angry, frustrated, defeated, and hurt. Dads may think, *Baby only wants Mom so why try?* A dad might not even respond to a child's crying because he thinks he cannot soothe the child anyway. This kind of self-talk that dads have in these moments is not biblical.

We are encouraging dads to think differently. We encourage you to praise the Lord that your baby loves his or her mom so much. Praise the Lord that he gave you an opportunity to show how wonderful his grace and love are in the midst of a hard moment. The baby did not stop crying, but you did care for him or her in a biblical way. Then, do it again the next day. Jealousy over Mom's seemingly magic touch will not help dads rest in God's grace, love the Lord more, or keep his commandments—especially the ones related to parenting.

We encourage dads to engage with their new baby and not allow cultural norms or prior experiences to thwart a strong relationship with their child. There will be times when the baby wants someone else—likely Mom. That is okay. The more dads engage and the more they are involved in each aspect of the parenting process, the more they may live out the gospel by walking worthy of their calling.

Exercises

1. Dads, ask the Lord to help you engage in the parenting process from the first day.

2. Have a conversation as a couple and try to think about some of the ways that Dad could be involved in the care of the baby (a few ideas are dropping off at day care, having a special Daddy snuggle time each day, or taking responsibility for one of the playtimes between feedings).

3. Have a conversation about how you plan to make decisions. There has to be some flexibility for one parent to simply make a choice, but there are other times where it is best to have involvement from both parents. What might be some of these times?

Chapter 10
All I Want Is "Me Time"

CARING FOR A new baby is delightful, but sometimes tiring work. Many moms and dads long for just a few moments of free time. Years ago, there was a commercial with the tagline, "Calgon, take me away." The final scene of the commercial was a woman taking a bubble bath without a care in the world. It represented a few moments of "me time." Other commercials showed a group of guys gathered to enjoy a great meal while watching their favorite sport. It also represented "me time."

Before baby arrived, most moms and dads were only responsible for themselves. For the most part, they decided when they were going to sleep. They decided when they were going to get up in the morning. Before the baby, moms and dads ate when they felt like eating. If they wanted to meet up with friends spontaneously or travel the world, then they had the liberty to do so. However, new moms and dads can expect a lot of change in their lives, exposing new areas of selfishness they might not have known they had.

The first forty-eight hours after delivery are generally spent recovering and bonding in the hospital. Those forty-eight hours are so special. Nurses will check on new mom and baby, offering help in many ways, and visitors may stop by to offer their encouragement. Adrenaline can fuel those first two days because new parents just want to hold their precious baby.

Generally speaking, babies sleep well during their first forty-eight hours of life. In fact, most first-time parents believe they have been given an easy-to-care-for baby based on those first two days. We thought that. Our firstborn was an angel in the hospital. We could not believe how easy he was. He hardly cried. *This is going to be easier than we had thought*, we told ourselves. Then, we took him home. And suddenly, he woke up. He was a totally different child at home than he was in the hospital.

In the early days and weeks, new babies will require much of your time, attention, and energy as they will be dependent on someone for everything. Nursing mothers will especially feel that burden. It seems that the cycle of feedings, diaper changes, playtime, and soothing a crying baby never stops. New moms often feel worn out, overwhelmed, and lonely. Dads also experience a similar emotion as they go to work on little, if any, sleep. There are moments when new parents might long for the good old days. They may remember those days where they were able to eat, sleep, and meet up with friends whenever they wanted. Those days when it was not difficult to find time to take a shower or read the Word of God.

At one point or another, most new moms and dads want some me time. I (Stephanie) have heard it expressed often among mothers, and I admit that I am guilty of both thinking and saying it a time or two when my own children were younger.

Is there any hope? Are there any gospel priorities that would help new parents who are struggling with the desire for some me time?

Let's begin by asking whether it is okay to desire some me time. The answer to that question cannot be addressed without thinking about heart motivations. What is so valuable about me time? We believe that physical and spiritual rest is very important.

Physical Rest

A new mom has a lot to do once her baby comes home from the hospital. Dad may have a few days off work, but it will not be long before he is working full-time. When he has normal work responsibilities, at least some of the household duties will belong to Mom, along with caring for many of the needs of her new baby. While the new responsibilities will be fun, they can also be exhausting. Over the years, I (Stephanie) have heard several new moms define a good day as one in which they were able to take a shower. This is especially true in the first few weeks as she is recovering and adjusting to a new schedule. There is a need to rest. God gave his people the Sabbath rest as a means of caring for his people (Exodus 20:8). Jesus also took moments of rest (see Mark 6:31 as one example).

With all the new responsibilities, it is helpful for a mom to take a nap or two during the day. It is not easy to get in a nap, but the best opportunity is during the time when your baby is sleeping or when your husband is home to care for the child. After all, it is hard to function on little sleep.

The lack of sleep is often a contributing factor to being grumpy, irritated, or unkind to others. This same idea could apply to dads. It may be that you helped with some nighttime duties and then had to leave for work with little sleep. For you, a weekend might be your best opportunity to find pockets of rest. Our point is that it is possible to work together so that each of you is able to rest to prepare for the ministry opportunities of the next day.

However, physical rest is not the only kind of rest that a new mom or dad needs. In fact, sometimes it is impossible to get that physical rest we so desire. In these cases, there is another kind of rest.

Spiritual Rest

A period of respite can be refreshing to not only the body, but also the soul. During busy times in life, people tend to shorten their time with the Lord. As I (Stephanie) recall some of my busy seasons in life, I can remember sitting on my couch trying to read the Word or pray. In my feeble efforts, I accomplished more dozing than reading. In those busy moments, believers need to be in the Word the most. They need to be communicating with the Lord on a regular basis.

Spiritual rest is not dependent on physical rest. There will be times when a nap does not remove your stress or worry. There will be times when physical rest just will not come and sleepless nights continue. Dad, you might feel like a zombie at work. Mom, you might feel like you cannot do another feeding. During these moments God meets us with a different kind of rest.

It is in the midst of these moments that God shows himself strong in our lives. It is in these moments that he empowers us to do his will. It is in these moments that we develop greater love for our child as we experience, in weakness, the great love of God. It is in these moments that we see God use us in the life of another person. One of our friends calls this time "baby boot camp."[5] It is a time that we experience God's strength in us during a time of weakness.

Scripture says that Jesus withdrew to solitary places for rest, for time alone to pray to his Father. In Luke 22:39–42, Jesus withdrew from his disciples while praying to his Father in the Garden of Gethsemane. In Matthew 14:13, upon hearing of the news that John the Baptist was killed, Jesus withdrew to a solitary place. Luke describes Jesus, saying, "But he would withdraw to desolate places and pray" (Luke 5:16). Ronald A. Beers commented on this passage,

---

5. We are thankful for Barbara Juliani's wonderful insight in personal communication about this section.

People were flocking to hear Jesus preach and to have their diseases healed, but Jesus made sure he often withdrew to quiet, solitary places to pray. Many things clamor for our attention, and we often run ourselves ragged attending to them. Like Jesus, however, we should take time to withdraw to a quiet and deserted place to pray. Strength comes from God and we can only be strengthened by spending time with him.[6]

Sometimes, what new parents need most is time with the Lord. It may be reading a few verses while feeding your child, or reading the Bible out loud to your baby during playtime, or listening to an audio Bible while you complete a chore. It is always a mind-set that looks to the Lord to give rest to the weary, strength to the weak, and hope to the hopeless. Consider what the Lord said through Isaiah in 40:28–31.

Have you not known? Have you not heard? The LORD is the everlasting God, the Creator of the ends of the earth. He does not faint or grow weary; his understanding is unsearchable. He gives power to the faint, and to him who has no might he increases strength. Even youths shall faint and be weary, and young men shall fall exhausted; but they who wait for the LORD shall renew their strength; they shall mount up with wings like eagles; they shall run and not be weary; they shall walk and not faint.

Isaiah prophesied the judgment that the Lord would bring upon the nation of Israel, but chapter 40 begins the section on

6. Ronald A. Beers, gen. ed. *Life Application Study Bible*, rev. ed (Grand Rapids: Zondervan, 1983), 1803.

redemption. God would discipline his people, but he was also going to redeem them. God is like no other. God never grows weary or tired, but he gives strength to the weary and power to the tired. Even young men reach a point where their strength fails, but not those who wait for the Lord.

Isaiah 40 is not about physical rest but spiritual rest. New parents need this rest, power, and strength that God provides. The Lord is faithful to new moms and dads. They will have strength they did not know was possible. Quiet time with God is a good form of me time.

A Selfish Me Time

Even a good desire can be a source of evil. Our goal in life is live for God's glory (1 Corinthians 10:31) and to praise his goodness (1 Peter 2:9). When a desire for rest, or pleasure, or comfort owns our heart, even good desires can be bad. James 4:1–3 explains this:

> What causes quarrels and what causes fights among you? Is it not this, that your passions are at war within you? You desire and do not have, so you murder. You covet and cannot obtain, so you fight and quarrel. You do not have, because you do not ask. You ask and do not receive, because you ask wrongly, to spend it on your passions.

James tells us that our inner desires compete. Sometimes we want rest more than we want Jesus. We want pleasure more than we want Jesus. These desires that become more important than the Lord take over our hearts and lead us into conflict. Sometimes a person asks God for something and God, who knows their hearts, refuses to give it because the request is for selfish purposes.

It is possible to make me time a desire over Jesus. Maybe we want time with friends, or time to ourselves, or time to do what we want to do. After all, new parents are occupied the first couple of months with the baby. During those months we can wonder about the number of wet diapers (because the doctor wants to know), whether the baby is eating enough, whether the baby is gaining weight, why the baby is crying, and what the baby's needs are. The list is practically endless. Sometimes new parents want their old life—where they could do what they want, when they want.

The issue is not being prepared to serve and care for others. Rather than asking the Lord how to receive rest so they can love the Lord and others more effectively (Matthew 22:37–40), they want to know when they can have time to spend solely on themselves.

Me time becomes wrong when there is a belief of entitlement. In other words, when moms or dads believe they are owed something or deserve something in exchange for taking care of the family. For example, because Mom is home all day by herself with the baby she believes that once Dad arrives home from work, it is time for a break and it is now his turn to have baby duty. Dad may say that he was up with the baby last night and now it is his wife's turn. There may be a place for these comments when the heart is right, but it is always possible that these comments are coming from an entitlement mentality. If so, Mom and Dad will miss the opportunity to see how God works in their tired state. They will miss seeing that by God's grace they could do more than they ever thought they could.

Entitlement could be possible if Mom is working full-time. The plan was to have Dad pick up the baby from childcare. However, at 3:30 p.m. Dad texts Mom to tell her that he has to work late and will not be able to pick up the baby. Mom just got more work than she was expecting. It would be easy to tell Dad that she had to do his work today (pick up the baby) so he is going to do hers tonight because she is done.

Our point is that me time should be replaced with the proper biblical category of rest. It is possible for either new moms or new dads, regardless of the working arrangements, to develop an entitlement philosophy in their heart that impacts how they treat one another. It is possible to convince ourselves that selfish me time is a biblical right. Instead, there is a legitimate place of physical and spiritual rest.

Paul writes, "Do nothing from rivalry or conceit, but in humility count others more significant than yourselves. Let each of you look not only to his own interests, but also to the interests of others" (Philippians 2:3–4). He emphasizes caring about others. Believers are called to think about others in a way that is higher than they think of themselves. That is no easy task, is it? What does this look like in practical terms as new parents?

As new parents care for their baby, they need to avoid complaining (Philippians 2:14). Lovingly and tenderly care for the baby's needs. Be thankful in all things (1 Thessalonians 5:18), even changing a diaper for the tenth time in one day or getting up for the third time during the night. Every sweet little baby grows into a walking and talking toddler. New parents may be tempted to say or think something like, *I can't even get a few minutes to myself in order to take a shower* or *I am half asleep at work every day* or *I get home and it is nothing but crying.* In moments such as this, new parents have an opportunity to humbly consider their little ones and their needs as more important than their own and to respond in a way that will bring honor and glory to God. In doing so, parents point their little ones to the gospel.

Philippians 2:5 emphasizes humility, following Jesus's example. Just as Jesus was humble so must his followers be humble. His humility in his incarnation, life, and death is to serve as an example.

One of the young moms in our church wrote this testimonial:[7]

> I struggle with the balance of wanting alone time in a
> biblical way versus a selfish way. Rest and alone time
> is not a bad thing since Jesus retreated to be alone and
> step away from the craziness. But quickly, my desires
> can turn selfish where I just want alone time to not be a
> mom/employee/wife in a selfish way because I just want
> to do what I want to do. I actually found it somewhat
> easier in the early days since my baby napped a lot as a
> newborn, so I had a lot of free time. I found it easier to
> use downtime to read my Bible and pray because I knew
> I would have other opportunities later in the day to do
> other things. Once returning to work, not having any
> sort of downtime (since his naps are when I'm at work)
> was a big struggle for me. I felt/feel like I deserve some
> relaxation after work and the nightly routines, but it is
> not necessarily always spiritual rest I desire. Trying to
> use little moments like my lunch break at work or my
> commute for spiritual rest is something I'm trying to
> grow in.

We appreciate this young mom's willingness to share her heart.
Having the proper balance in this area can be a challenge as new
parents wrestle with needing spiritual rest and wanting alone time
to do what they enjoy doing. Sometimes new parents may need to
redefine what me time looks like, just as our sweet friend is doing.
Her desire to use her lunch break and commute for spiritual rest
can help her be in a better position to joyfully care for the needs

---

7. For the sake of context, this mom had a couple months off her paid job immediately after their child was born. She returned to her workplace when the baby was three
months old.

of her family. With God's help, new parents can please him in this area of their life, they can see God's provision even when they are exhausted and weary, and they are more prepared to be effective servants of Christ.

As you care for your child and each other it will properly prepare you for the remainder of your life. Those of us who have gone through these stages of life can testify that caring for babies produced quality fruit in our lives. It made us stronger and more confident that God's grace abounds in our sin, in our suffering, and in our dependence on him.

Exercises

1. Explain to each other the difference between physical and spiritual rest. Talk about one or two instances where you tried to apply the wrong solution to the type of rest you needed.

2. Discuss one or two ways that you will attempt to get physical and spiritual rest (or make it easy to get them).

3. Put your favorite passage about rest on an index card and review it weekly.

Chapter 11

Sexual Intimacy
as a New Parent

ONE AREA OF the marriage relationship we did not address in the earlier chapters is sexual intimacy. You will build relational intimacy as you work together, become a team, love your new baby together, and appreciate the other's contributions. If you will work on your part and rely on the Lord's strength, then your relationship will be significantly stronger. We have yet, however, to address the issue of sexual intimacy. This chapter will seek to encourage both spouses immediately after your baby is born.[8]

I (Rob) cannot remember where exactly I heard the phrase "skin time" for the first time, but as soon as I heard it, the phrase made sense. Skin time refers to the skin-on-skin contact that can benefit a newborn. Often, moms or dads place their newborn on their bare chest. Our son grew from the size of one cell to an almost eight-pound infant inside Stephanie's womb. For nine months our baby's entire world was the size of my wife's body. After the very rude awakening of delivery, the sound of her heartbeat and the touch of her warm skin was very comforting. Many dads realize that the notion of skin time will also apply to them.

---

8. Prior to delivery, couples will continue to follow the guidelines found in chapter 8 of *Tying the Knot* (Rob Green, *Tying the Knot*, Greensboro, NC: New Growth Press, 2016).

As delivery day approaches, new moms can be uncomfortable. The child is nearing full term and while the feeling of a child in her womb is often wonderful, it can be challenging as well. Some couples will experience a short time of celibacy prior to birth because sexual intercourse is not very enjoyable. Many couples find other forms of sexual expression, intimacy, or closeness satisfying and relationship building.

The advice we received—and it was largely the experience of others we know—was to wait six weeks after birth before resuming sexual intimacy, to give Mom time to heal from the delivery. I (Rob) admit that I had never watched a delivery before my son was born. We went to the class at the hospital, but I either conveniently missed that day or found something else to occupy my mind. I happily watched my children's births, but I had zero interest in being there under any other circumstances. Delivery was beautiful, but we both had a new appreciation for Genesis 3:16 (in pain you shall bring forth children). In addition, delivery was a time to offer thankfulness for her sacrifice.

During this prolonged period without sexual intercourse, there are important gospel priorities for husbands. For example, new dads are to love their wives as Christ loves the church (Ephesians 5:25–26). Remember that sex is for the glory of God and for the mutual benefit (1 Corinthians 7:2–3). If sex would not be loving or enjoyable for her, then patience is the appropriate response. Stewardship also dictates that new dads spend much time and energy caring for the helpless child God gave us. Further, our identity and joy is found in the one who gives spiritual life and provides every resource of mercy and grace (1 Peter 2:9–10), the one who will give you the patience you need. It seems simple, right?

Sexual desire and intimacy may be an issue after the required waiting period is over. Many men understand the need to pause before and for a period of time after the birth. However, it is possible to think that the six-week doctor checkup is the turning point in sexual relations. If a wife is not equally interested then it is possible for conflict to arise. Sometimes men start wondering when they will get "skin time" too. It is here that the battle for a gospel-centered, Jesus-centered approach to sexual relations can begin.

New dads who know their Bibles can even use Scripture to explain their desire, "Do not deprive one another, except perhaps by agreement for a limited time, that you may devote yourselves to prayer, but then come together again, so that Satan will not tempt you because of your lack of self-control" (1 Corinthians 7:5). If a husband has been patient and loving about the pause in sexual relations, he may now believe that he is owed this, or that he is being deprived. The thought is that it is now his wife's responsibility to care about his desires for sexual expression. A new dad might hope for a return to gospel passages like those found in the Song of Solomon.

Further, a physician's clearance for sex does not necessarily mean that sexual intercourse will be immediately comfortable. Some ladies will heal faster than others. Some births are easier than others. This can add a layer of frustration to the experience to one or both spouses.

To make matters worse, it is possible for a new dad to assume that sex post-delivery will be just like it was before delivery. This is not always the case, especially if Mom is nursing. For some women the stimulation of the breast during sexual play is similar to the stimulation used to prepare for nursing. The feeling of milk letting down can even occur if a mom hears her baby crying. It is how God has designed her body. With a first child, those experiences are new. While some women might enjoy that experience, others may struggle.

Babies also can be distracting. It is not difficult to imagine a scenario where the baby is asleep and a couple decides to engage in sexual play when suddenly the baby awakes and begins crying. Again, this is a new experience. Prior to having a child, the couple could silence their electronic devices and devote a period of time to pleasing one another. Babies cannot be placed on silent. If the couple had planned for this sexual experience in advance, then one or both could be angry that the child interrupted and potentially changed the plans for the entire evening.

When you put these things together, it is not hard to see that bringing a child into the world can have implications for a couple's sexual relationship that need gospel-centered responses.

Gospel Truth for Husbands

The Lord gives husbands joy, satisfaction, and contentment. The book of Philippians is known, in part, for the number of times that Paul emphasizes joy. Paul is writing while being imprisoned for his faith. Despite those circumstances, he has contentment, joy, and satisfaction. Paul's circumstances do not determine his contentment or joy. Rather, Paul receives his joy by partnering in the gospel with Jesus and other believers. When husbands are focused on the gospel and the partnership with their wife to raise a child, then they may spend less time focused on their perceived needs not being met.

Philippians 4:13 explains that contentment is possible because God's strength serves as the source of contentment, joy, and satisfaction. Paul says, "I can do all things through him who strengthens me." There is nothing wrong with husbands desiring their wives sexually, but sex is not the foundation of contentment and joy. Those are found in Christ first, and then in the various ways that husbands glorify him. If meaningful sexual expression is difficult, then husbands have the opportunity to focus on their ultimate joy and satisfaction—the person of Christ.

Loving and caring for others is a God-given privilege. Sometimes, it is easy to forget that parenting is a wonderful privilege. It is wise to give thanks to the Lord for the blessing of parenting.

Husbands are called to love their wives as Christ loved the church (Ephesians 5:25). This command applies equally to the time before and after a child is born. The husband is called to give and sacrifice for his wife just as Christ did for the church. The presence of a child may provide him with more opportunity to do so. We encourage new fathers not to nag or mope around the house. Instead, love your wife, care for her, love the new baby, and care for the new baby even if it means that sexual expression is infrequent or disappointing.

The Lord provides strength in temptation. One of the greatest tools of manipulation that men use against their wives is the issue of temptation. Part of the challenge is that Scripture is clear that when we deprive one another we open a door for Satan's temptations. That is a point to be made. However—and it is a big however—facing temptation does not require giving in to that temptation.

Some men say that they would not have committed adultery, looked at pornography, masturbated, or participated in some other sinful sexual expression if their wife had satisfied them. This is nothing short of self-centered manipulation and blame shifting.

Scripture instead exhorts, "No temptation has overtaken you that is not common to man. God is faithful, and he will not let you be tempted beyond your ability, but with the temptation he will also provide the way of escape, that you may be able to endure it" (1 Corinthians 10:13).

The Lord, in his grace, is faithful to ensure that even Satan is properly limited. God will provide a path to escape sin as a person endures temptation. If the sexual part of a couple's relationship is moving slower than the husband desires, they can still have complete confidence that God will help them endure whatever temptation they face.

If you are reading this book and you have struggled with giving in to sexual sin, we encourage you to seek additional help from your pastor or church leaders. God may use this time of abstinence to teach you lessons about his grace, his presence, his discipline, and how to avoid temptation. The fight against sin involves your relationship with Jesus, the kind of accountability you are willing to accept, your willingness to look at sin in its ugly horrors, and the lengths you will go to in order to make no provision for your flesh (Romans 13:14). Your best plan might be to humble yourself and ask for help.

A time of waiting can be a great opportunity for God to show you his power and faithfulness. God may reveal more of his character and glory as he bids husbands to trust him and mature in their character.

The Lord uses circumstances for good. Romans 8:28–29 is a passage frequently used to describe the difficult circumstances Christians experience. During trials believers often question God, and this passage reminds them that God uses all circumstances, including the ones they would not normally choose, to make them more like Christ. It reads, "And we know that for those who love God all things work together for good, for those who are called according to his purpose. For those whom he foreknew he also predestined to be conformed to the image of his Son, in order that he might be the firstborn among many brothers" (Romans 8:28–29).

We encourage fathers and husbands to see their situation through the lens of a faithful and caring God who is making them more like Christ. A wife not being ready for sex as quickly as a husband is not a crisis. It is one way that the Lord may grow husbands into more effective lovers of the Lord and of the people in their lives.

If you are a man who struggles wanting sexual intimacy and it is your wife who is requesting greater frequency, then the same passages apply but with a different application. Loving your wife would mean being willing to satisfy her sexually even if you would rather not. There still is a battle with temptation, but the temptation is for you to withhold from her. There still is the fact that God uses this trial to help you become more like Christ.

A Word to Wives from a Wife

Ladies, just as your husband needs to handle his sexual desires in a Christ-centered and gospel-centered manner, you have to do the same. The type of delivery you have impacts how quickly you heal and are ready to enjoy intercourse again. Some of you may be very interested in your husband quickly; others of you may be less enthusiastic. Christ helps you as well. The question I (Stephanie) want to answer is how wives can love and encourage their husbands after a longer period of celibacy than normal or when the desire for sex between a husband and wife does not match, or when additional time is needed for healing.

Be a good communicator. Ephesians 4:29 says, "Let no corrupting talk come out of your mouths, but only such as is good for building up, as fits the occasion, that it may give grace to those who hear." You and your husband may have a wonderful relationship, but he is not able to read your mind or physically feel what you are feeling. Even though you may be tired from the care of your baby, your husband will still need words that are good for building up. Please also notice that our words need to fit the occasion. If your husband expresses interest in sex and you are not interested, then it is wise to communicate that with him. When you communicate do not speak about unrelated subjects like grocery shopping, what the baby did, or what you are planning to wear the next day. Instead, speak clearly about your lack of interest in sex using words that still fit in the definition given in Ephesians 4:29. You might say something like, "Love, I am so glad you are interested in me, and I am interested in you too. Today, however, I am still very sore. Even though I am not physically ready for intercourse could we lie in bed and snuggle together?" Ladies, this tells your husband that you are interested in him, which shows him that you care about him, you are being honest about your physical situation, and you offer an alternative. Ladies, please communicate wisely and appropriately with your husband.

Be willing to take further steps as appropriate. If you have been cleared by your physician and intercourse would not be damaging in any way, you should consider making attempts at intercourse. Women may need a few tries to feel as comfortable as they did prior to delivery, but that is okay. It might be that you can make an attempt. If you are not ready, then relax and communicate with your husband that more time is needed. Recovery can be longer than six weeks, and there is no need to feel guilty over being sore. If you are not ready for intercourse, consider sexual play or "skin time" instead.

If you are a woman who wants more sexual intimacy than your husband, please be patient with him. He might be concerned about hurting you. He might be concerned about having another baby right way. Whatever the reason, it might be that your man is still processing being a husband and a father. A little patience might be more loving than pushing him for sex.

Be attentive to your husband. I (Stephanie) have heard from several ladies that they are "touched out" by the end of the day when caring for their newborn. This is especially true for ladies who are breastfeeding. By the end of the day, they want their space, and they do not want to share that space with anyone else, not even their husband. I encourage ladies not to allow their child to be an excuse to neglect their husbands. Instead, they should seek to be attentive to their husband's sexual interests. Again, if you are a woman who is more interested than your husband, you can be attentive to him by gently and patiently encouraging him to express more interest.

Sex is an important part of marriage, but it is not the only part or even the most important part. After a baby is born it is possible that the husband and wife will not have the same desire for sexual expression. Remembering the call to love Christ and the reality that Christ has provided spiritual resources may help you both put sex in its proper perspective.

Exercises

1. Pray and ask the Lord to help you think biblically about your sexual desires during this life stage.

2. Memorize the passage of Scripture that will most help you focus on gospel truth in the area of sex and encourage you to live a contented, satisfied, and joyful life for Christ.

3. Meet with one or two other godly parents who would be willing to give you advice for how to handle some of these moments after the baby is born.

Chapter 12

Learning to Teach and Discipline

THE VAST MAJORITY of this resource has been geared to helping new parents prepare and respond well to the infant stage of parenting. However, the infant stage will pass quickly, and parents will soon need to teach and discipline a toddler. There are many helpful books on these topics. This chapter cannot cover the entire range of parenting. Our goals for this chapter are much more modest. We want to think with you what it means for a parent to provide instruction and discipline to their child. We know that parents need to teach and discipline. Deuteronomy 6:6–7 tells parents that they should be continually teaching, "And these words that I command you today shall be on your heart. You shall teach them diligently to your children, and shall talk of them when you sit in your house, and when you walk by the way, and when you lie down, and when you rise."

Every event is a potential teachable moment. Deuteronomy emphasizes how teaching is an attitude of the home. The importance of God's Word as the content for teaching is clarified in Psalm 119:9–11. It says, "How can a young man keep his way pure? By guarding it according to your word. With my whole heart I seek you; let me not wander from your commandments! I have stored up your word in my heart, that I might not sin against you." Teaching children God's Word is required for us and them to live gospel-centered lives. The culture of a God-honoring home will have Jesus and his Word front and center.

Parents also need to discipline their children. The Lord expects Christian parents to teach and discipline their children for his honor and glory and to encourage children to understand the God of heaven and earth. Understanding this concept and being able to put it into practice was something we had to learn. We hope that this chapter will help you as prepare to do both.

Learning to Teach

Parents are always teaching their children through their own behavior. As babies grow, they begin to understand what their parents are saying and can respond to requests and commands.

We are going to discuss how parents can teach their children from the perspective of content, time, and awareness of understanding.

Content

God's Word forms the foundation of the content that parents teach their children. We encourage parents to talk to their children about the character of God and their need for Christ. Even when their child is a baby, new parents should be communicating that God is always good and that he is always gracious. Moses writes,

> The LORD passed before him and proclaimed, "The LORD, the LORD, a God merciful and gracious, slow to anger, and abounding in steadfast love and faithfulness, keeping steadfast love for thousands, forgiving iniquity and transgression and sin, but who will by no means

clear the guilty, visiting the iniquity of the fathers on the children and the children's children, to the third and the fourth generation." (Exodus 34:6–7)

Telling children these truths can be a good reminder to parents, but it may also set in motion the precedent that talking about God is normal. Parents help their children understand who God is early in the child's life. Will your child hear you talking about the steadfast love of the Lord? Will they hear you talk about God's forgiveness? Will they envision a God who is waiting for you to do something wrong so he can execute his wrath, or will they learn about the loving God who solved a problem that you could not solve?

Will your children hear about Jesus, both his first coming where he died on the cross and his second coming when he will fulfill all his promises? Will your children hear about their sin and their need for him? As children age, the opportunities for gospel presentations become more frequent. In the meantime, you have the chance to lay the groundwork for why your children need the true God.

Parents can also teach their children about their hearts. People cannot fully know their own hearts, but they can learn categories like behavior, emotion, motivation, and affection. While these categories are all intertwined into one dynamic heart, children can learn basic differences between these functions. For example, *affection* refers to what a person loves. Even little children can understand that they love being in control or they love doing whatever they want. Behavior describes what a person does. Even little children can understand that their parents are concerned not only with what they do, but also with what they worship or love. Human hearts worship, even little ones. The sooner and more frequently parents are talking about worship, the better. *Motivation* describes the reasons why we choose to do something. Children need to learn about motivation—they do not normally understand their motivations without loving guidance.

As an example, when a little child loves the joy that their things (toys, clothes, bed) bring them, they become more protective of them. They can get upset if a sibling or another person touches their things. This is an opportunity to talk about their hearts. You can speak about what they love, the motive to protect what they love, and the actions they take to keep what they love from someone else.

Parents can teach their children about love. Learning to love God and love others is not natural. Instead, it is easy to focus on oneself. Even little children can be told that the world does not revolve around them, but instead that God designed them to love and care about him and others. Parents can find simple ways for toddlers to love others (like learning to dress themselves, or put their dirty clothes in a basket, or pick up their toys). To go back to our earlier example, once they examine their hearts, they can see that sharing their toys or their clothes is a loving action to take in order to care for another person.

Another early example is sharing food. To model sharing, Stephanie and I would share something at the table with each other and with our children. Then we would ask our children to share with us. (Full disclosure: if you choose to use food to teach sharing, be prepared because sometimes you get a little more than the food!)

Parents can teach their children about authority. We encourage you to explain that God has provided authorities to help, grow, and protect children. These authorities will be appropriate for a child's age.[9]

Much more could be said about content, but the key observation is to see that the teaching is about spiritual matters—the character of God, his grace, the finished work of Christ, love for others,

---

9. We have all heard stories of older children or adults taking advantage of their authority in order to abuse a child. We encourage you to properly vet anyone who will have responsibility for your children. As the child grows, you also teach them what is appropriate and inappropriate touching and to tell you if someone violates this. Of course, pray that God would protect them from evil and the evil one.

and authority. While many of these will not be clear to an infant or young toddler, parents are establishing the pattern of talking about the Lord on a regular basis.

Time

According to Deuteronomy 6, instruction is provided all the time. Every moment is a teachable moment. Parents can embrace their responsibility to teach when those moments occur—and if they do, they will provide a lot of teaching. These moments are opportunities to help children see the significance of Christ. Let us offer two comments. First, our exhortation shows how important your relationship with Christ is in the process of parenting. You cannot give what you do not have. Second, it is tempting not to offer this kind of teaching. It is time consuming, and after a long day it can be challenging to be mentally ready for these constant opportunities.

Awareness of Understanding

By about a year of age children will respond to a request for a kiss. Even though they cannot speak yet, they understand what a kiss is, and they attempt to give it—slobber and all. They may respond to a comment like, "Where is daddy?" They will begin looking for Daddy. It is clear that they understand what others are saying because they choose the appropriate actions. Children can grow in their understanding, but it often comes slowly and over time.

Just because parents teach something does not mean children understand it. Please read that again. This was a hard lesson for us. We falsely assumed that our teaching resulted in their understanding. We learned from the school of hard knocks. Understanding the difference between parental teaching and a child understanding is particularly difficult during the ages of about nine months to three or four years old. By the time children turn four, they normally have enough vocabulary and enough ability to communicate that parents can learn whether the child understands simply by asking them. However, from the time children move (normally around nine months) until they have command of the language, it is difficult to understand whether they know.

Once our children were eating solid food, we told them they had two choices with their food. They could eat it, or they could leave it on their tray. They were not allowed to throw it, give it to the dog, or drop it on the floor. Admittedly, we did not know whether our little one was being defiant and rebellious or whether our little one did not really understand our request. After all, throwing food brings a certain amount of pleasure. When our kids gave food to the dog, the dog immediately reinforced that behavior. How do parents know when their child understands?

What about climbing the stairs? We are fairly adventurous people, but as young parents, we knew that stairs could be too much for our little one. The risk of injury far outweighed the joy of adventure (at least for a while). As a result, we did not want our children climbing or descending stairs without one of us present, until they were coordinated enough to do it safely. Yet those stairs are like magnets. How do parents know when their child is curious and when they are rebelling?

Here are three signs that we looked for to judge whether our children understood our requests or whether our words still had no clear referent.

1. Could both Stephanie and I remember times when we heard each other give instructions? The first sign is on us. We are the adults. Responsibility for teaching begins with us. If either of us could not articulate the commands, then it was highly unlikely that our child could either.

2. Does the child return after our third or fourth attempt to redirect them? We were looking for repetition. Our child, for example, crawled to the stairs and started climbing. One of us picks up our

little one, moves him to a new location, explains that the stairs are dangerous and off limits, and provides a distracting toy. What happens next? Are they distracted? Or are they right back at the stairs? If parents go through this process three or four times, they have much more confidence that their children know exactly what they are doing. Their confidence is not certain because children develop by doing, but repetition is one indication of understanding.

3. The look of guilt right before the action. This was our clearest sign. If our little one was sitting in their high chair eating, stopped, looked us, and then with a little grin took a Cheerio and tossed it across the room, we had a pretty good idea that was no accident. Or when our little one went to the wall outlet and looked at us prior to touching it, we believed he knew he was disobeying us.

These guidelines also remind parents of their dependence on the Lord. Each of these signs could be something other than rebellion. It is always possible that a smile and a tossed Cheerio are not closely connected. The smile is for you, the Cheerio for fun. This requires us to regularly ask the Lord to give us the wisdom that comes from above.

The Lord gives parents the privilege of teaching their children. Teaching is a skill, and not all parents have an awareness of teaching. Just because parents say something does not mean that children have grasped it. We believe it is helpful to look for signs of knowledge. This could be true of older children as well, but the ability to use language makes testing understanding easier.

Correcting Lack of Understanding

First, when there is a lack of understanding, there is the need to teach. Parents often teach lessons multiple ways at multiple times. Some children learn a concept faster than others. Treat children according to their ability to understand.

Second, learning to teach often reminds parents of their dependency on Christ. There will be times when parents are not sure how to communicate truth in a way that is meaningful and helpful. Parents should always be humble, knowing that they are dependent on the grace of Christ to do anything meaningful.

Third, once children understand the expectation, then parents are in a position to hold them accountable to that expectation. Parents can be slow, thoughtful, and repetitive, but there comes a time for accountability. Once children know, it is the parents' responsibility to hold them accountable to their knowledge. When children choose the path of rebellion, the choice becomes an opportunity to share their need for a savior.

Parents have the privilege of teaching their children. While those in the church can help and those in the school systems will also play a role, it is important to remember that parents are accountable. They cannot delegate that responsibility to anyone else. Focusing on teaching the right content, applying that content to various life circumstances, and thoughtfully evaluating children's understanding may help parents honor the Lord.

Learning to Discipline

In addition to learning to teach, parents also have the task of disciplining their children.

Before we became parents, there were certain aspects of discipline that seemed clear to us. We thought the concept of discipline was clear. We were trying to help our child learn that something needed to change. That "something" may be a behavior, an attitude, or a way of thinking. Discipline is helping the child to understand that something has to be different.

Second, we understood that discipline was redemptive in purpose. It was not revenge, not "You created this inconvenience for me and now I am going to create an inconvenience for you." Discipline was to direct the child toward the greater spiritual needs as well as addressing the direct behavior.

Third, we understood that discipline could involve a number of different possibilities. Discipline can include removing a privilege; it can be a time for children to think on their own; it can be corporal punishment; it can be completing a special task—like doing an additional chore or writing out a passage of Scripture and explaining what obedience to that text would have looked like. We understood that discipline included lots of options.

What we did not understand was how hard those things are to do in the moment. We believe that understanding precedes discipline. If a parent is unsure whether a child understands their request, then the proper action is to teach again. In our judgment, parents should keep teaching until they have evidence for understanding. Knowing exactly when to teach and when to discipline can be tricky. Once there is understanding, parents must address rebellion consistently. Here are a few tips we learned the hard way.

Discipline is easier when implemented early and maintained.

As new parents we did not think a lot about the little ways of rebellion our children exhibited. We too quickly blamed it on a stage or part of being a child. For example, one of our children had to be moved from a crib to a bed because one day he climbed out on his own. We believed that this was curiosity, and we moved him to a normal bed so he would not get hurt. Then, he would get up during his nap time and get out all his toys. He would get up at night and make a mess despite repeated instructions. All too often, we blamed this on "what two-year-olds do." This was unwise. We can remember learning more about discipline when our first child was about four years old. We disciplined in the past, but we also allowed for a lot of rebellion. When we decided that the Lord would be honored by dealing with the rebellion, it was not easy. Our child had learned how to manipulate us and did not appreciate losing that ability.

By God's grace, we learned when our first was still young, but we have a counseling ministry that regularly serves families with difficult children. Sometimes, those children became difficult due to their own sinful and rebellious choices without the fault of the parents. But other times, the parents provided a culture where rebellion could thrive and grow. We encourage parents to start early and to remember the many types of discipline. In the early days, discipline can be as simple as moving children in order to redirect their attention (with a conversation as to why).

Discipline is consistent but not always perfect.

We heard that the parents always need to win. That sounded great until we had children. It seemed like one day our child would be obedient and easy to parent, and then the next day, it seemed we were ineffective with discipline. There were days when we went to bed thinking that our children had completely dominated us. Win? We barely survived.

We had to remember that discipline is not always perfect, and it does not always give immediate results. We had to remember that parenting is war. It is a war for the heart and life of our child. This statement may sound bold, but we started using it after we were parents. Every day brought new opportunities, and every day we had to be ready. Scripture tells us that the devil is like a roaring lion seeking someone to devour (1 Peter 5:8). Devour? Strong words. Ephesians 6:12 says that our struggling, wrestling, or fighting is against spiritual forces, which is why we need the full armor of God (Ephesians 6:11). Parenting is a task for warriors. Even if there were days when we felt defeated and frustrated, we knew that God would provide enough strength for the new day. We needed to go to bed and line up our forces for war in the morning.

We wish we could have achieved perfect parenting. We realized we could not. What we could do was be consistent.

Discipline only works when God is also at work.

We have heard expectations such as, "obedience with a happy heart." While this may be a goal, many adults do not respond to the Lord's discipline in their lives in this way either (Hebrews 12:5–11). Sometimes parents have to settle for obedience, knowing that there is more work to be done on the heart.

It would be wonderful if the three-year-old came to Mom and Dad to say, "I sinned against the Lord and you in terrible ways. I did not listen and chose my own path because my heart is more wicked than I even know. I need my heart cleansed. I have spent the last thirty minutes begging for the Lord's forgiveness and I am clinging to the fact that he has forgiven me. Now I am asking for your forgiveness. I know that with repentance comes the willingness to accept the consequences that you believe are righteous and just, and I am prepared to accept them." This scenario, however, it not realistic. Adults do not often repent like that.

We were told that parents can bring their children to the point of "obedience with a happy heart," but it was a false goal. We could not attain it. At their very best, parents bring a child to obedience. The happy heart comes as the Lord works mightily in a person, developing love and affection.

Spending ten minutes with God asking for his work may better prepare parents for the discipline moment. We suggested that dependence on the Lord is required for understanding, for teaching, for discipline, and for discipline to be effective. Parents, this type of praying is what Paul describes in Colossians 4:2, "continue steadfastly in prayer." As you see the rebellious nature of your child coming out, pray for God to turn that child toward Jesus. As you struggle with seeing results from your discipline, ask the Lord to help you persevere, but also to know how you could discipline in a more godly fashion. Yes, parenting is war, but it is not a battle you fight on your own.

What else can help? We do not have a perfect list, but here are a few things that helped us in our journey of living out Ephesians 6:4 in a meaningful way.

The discipline needs to occur while understanding is present.

It would be nice if every rebellious act happened within the four walls of our home. That was not the case. For example, if our little one decided to express sinful anger at the store or at another person's home, then we had to decide what to do. We wanted to be sure that our discipline could be connected to the event that warranted the discipline. Sometimes that meant our discipline changed.

Be wise and thoughtful with discipline.

Old Testament law prescribed different penalties for different types of lawbreaking. There was a provision for intentional lawbreaking and one for lawbreaking by accident. We found both of these concepts helpful. They reminded us that we did not have to apply the same solution to every problem. Some offenses were more serious than others and thus warranted a more serious response.

Ensure both parents are involved in discipline.

This may not sound like an important matter in infancy, but it will bear fruit in the future. As children grow, they figure out if Mom and Dad are together. They learn which one is more likely to give them what they want. They learn to play Mom and Dad against one another. One of the ways parents ensure that does not happen is with consistent discipline from both parents.

Be prepared to discipline.

Parents can bring whatever discipline they choose in a way that is controlled, goal-oriented, and purposeful. Parents may find it helpful, in some circumstances, to pray and read Scripture prior to discipline so that all discipline is done in a controlled fashion. We can be thankful that Hebrews 12:5–11 describes the way the Lord disciplines his children. Our heavenly father is always controlled, giving us exactly the right, loving discipline.

Discipline opportunities are also designed to point everyone involved to Christ. Parents need Christ so that their discipline is appropriate, showing the relationship between their behavior and heart to the Lord, and with clear instructions on what a proper heart and obedience would look like in the next situation. Children must also see that the goal is to help them learn more about Jesus and what it looks like to live for him.

Words about Abuse

We wish that we did not have to mention the word *abuse* in this book. Sadly, we live in a world where abuse happens. State protection agencies are often overrun with cases of abuse, and occasionally we learn of a case through the national news. There are times when men abuse women, times when women abuse men, and other times that parents or stepparents abuse children. While we wish this issue only occurred in homes outside the church, the reality is that abuse happens in homes inside the church as well. We want to remind you that abuse is sin and against all that God has designed the parent-child relationship to be. While some individuals create a culture of abuse, others abuse in a moment of anger gone wild. All instances of abuse are wrong. They are violations of God's Word and the law.

We do not want to unnecessarily scare you as expecting parents, but we do want to warn you. If you experienced abuse as a child, we encourage you to speak with one of your pastors or leaders in order to give some special attention to your spiritual care and how to individually prepare for children of your own. If you are being abused yourself, then please contact the appropriate authorities and church leaders to receive physical protection and spiritual help.

Exercises

1. Discuss with your spouse what you believe the most helpful observations were from this chapter. Please put two of them on an index card and put them near the crib.

2. Discuss the kinds of discipline that you experienced and what you might want to avoid or implement as parents yourselves. What do you think will be the hardest aspect of discipline for you? Why?

3. Think about your first year with a new child. What truths would you like to teach (for example, Mommy and Daddy love you, Jesus loves you more than Mommy and Daddy, the Bible is God's Word)? What kind of discipline would you employ at this early stage?

4. Write out characteristics of a home where Jesus is the center. How would you compare that with homes where the children are the center? What about a home where the parent is the center?

Chapter 13

Cast Your Cares on God

WE BELIEVE THAT you can be a godly. You can raise children in the nurture and admonition of the Lord. We believe that God cares and will help. We believe that the Lord invites you to rely on him. First Peter 5:6–7 say, "Humble yourselves, therefore, under the mighty hand of God so that at the proper time he may exalt you, casting all your anxieties on him, because he cares for you." Let us consider some of the ways that God genuinely cares.

God Provides Grace and Mercy

The author of Hebrews reminds us,

> Since then we have a great high priest who has passed through the heavens, Jesus, the Son of God, let us hold fast our confession. For we do not have a high priest who is unable to sympathize with our weaknesses, but one who in every respect has been tempted as we are, yet without sin. Let us then with confidence draw near to the throne of grace, that we may receive mercy and find grace to help in time of need. (Hebrews 4:14–16)

Jesus, as the high priest, knows how to sympathize with new parents' weaknesses. It is true that Jesus was not a biological parent. Yet one of the great privileges that believers enjoy is to call God their "Father" or "Abba, Father." This demonstrates that the Lord is fully aware of the challenges with parenting. It is encouraging that parents can approach God, who can genuinely sympathize with their struggles.

Christ was also able to handle the various trials and temptations without sin. It is encouraging that new parents can lean on a person who knows how to handle difficulty. It reminds new parents of the promise given in 1 Corinthians 10:13 that God provides a way to endure trials without giving into sin.

God gives receive mercy and grace in the time of need. New parents confidently come to God's throne because the Lord wants them to come and because the Lord has the resources to help. Thankfully, the invitation is not restricted to a particular time and place. Thus, whether parents are driving to work at seven-thirty in the morning or whether they are in the nursery at three in the morning, there is grace and mercy available. We found this very comforting and one of the ways that we knew God always cares for us.

God Promises Never to Leave

Again, the author of Hebrews encourages us, "Keep your life free from love of money, and be content with what you have, for he has said, 'I will never leave you nor forsake you.' So we can confidently say, 'The Lord is my helper; I will not fear; what can man do to me?'" (Hebrews 13:5–6).

The author writes to a group of people who have suffered. They lost their homes and were forced to relocate (Hebrews 10:32–34). It would have been easy to place some of their hope in money. The argument of Hebrews 13 is that hope, security, and contentment come in knowing that God is always near. No matter what people experience, they can be sure that God will never forsake them. We believe new parents will experience moments of feeling alone or feeling like they are at their wit's end. It will be in those moments that the presence of Christ can encourage, comfort, and remind them that they are never alone.

Trials, difficulties, confusion, and challenge lead us to question whether the Lord is with us. David even wrote in Psalm 13 that it appeared the Lord had left him and was no longer with him. This is part of the human experience. Psalm 13 ends with an assurance that the Lord is good to David, but only after he continually seeks God's presence and deliverance. Just as it was true for David, God will never leave you or forsake you.

This was a particularly helpful concept to us when our first child was born. Eight weeks earlier, we had moved five hundred miles. We left our church family, whom we knew well, and both sets of loving families. The home we left was in a decent-sized city, and our apartment was less than two hundred yards from a major interstate. We moved into the country. Our first night, without window coverings up yet, was darker than any night we had experienced in years. Since we had a baby only eight weeks later and we had not yet established ourselves as part of a community, God's presence reminded us that we were never alone.

God Gives a Loving Community of Encouragement

Hebrews continues to encourage us, saying, "Let us hold fast the confession of our hope without wavering, for he who promised is faithful. And let us consider how to stir up one another to love and good works, not neglecting to meet together, as is the habit of some, but encouraging one another, and all the more as you see the Day drawing near" (Hebrews 10:23–25).

The church is a loving community. It is a place where believers encourage one another to love and good deeds. It is a place where believers retreat from the world for a bit as they gather together to study the Word and worship corporately. These are important elements in the health of any believer, but there is more.

Community gives new parents the opportunity to serve and to be served. Both elements are important components to the Christian life. As new parents have needs, it is helpful and encouraging to know that their friends care. Community is there to give love and perform good deeds, which result in blessing and encouragement. Serving is equally important. As a part of the community, new parents contribute as well as receive. The community exists to encourage new parents to love others and to perform acts of kindness. Serving is crucial to spiritual health. We remind the couples we counsel that every believer gets to the place where learning another truth will only produce fruit if it finds an outward expression. Believers are exhorted to be both hearers of the word and doers (James 1:22–23).

It is tempting to isolate oneself in the midst of major life changes like marriage, a first baby, and moving away from family for the first time. New parents don't need to isolate themselves from the community. They can still serve. New parents can make meals for other new parents, visit people who are ill, attend community activities, and care for other's children. Community can be one of the ways new parents experience God caring for them.

God Provides Wisdom

James encourages, "If any of you lacks wisdom, let him ask God, who gives generously to all without reproach, and it will be given him" (James 1:5).

The larger context of James 1 discusses trials. While Christians do not ask for trials, we believe that God uses trials to make believers more mature. We have never met a person, let alone a parent, who has never faced trials and suffering of some kind. The world is waiting for redemption just as people are awaiting final redemption. Thus, the world contains suffering. Some of that suffering intersects everyone's life. Sometimes trials are much more personal. It could be a complication during or after birth with Mom or baby. It could be an injury that occurs. It is almost certain that there will be something. When that "something" comes, believers know that asking for wisdom is possible. Christians know that in the quietness of the hard moments, they can humble themselves before the Lord and ask for his help. They can believe that God will give them the wisdom that is necessary to deal with the trial.

In fact, the text says that God gives wisdom generously. When Solomon chose wisdom (1 Kings 3), God was so pleased with his request that God gave wisdom and blessing. Sometimes believers are slow to ask the Lord because he does not necessarily answer immediately. The problem is not the desire for wisdom, but the demand that wisdom be given immediately.

God Prays for His People

Paul encourages believers, saying,

> Likewise the Spirit helps us in our weakness. For we do not know what to pray for as we ought, but the Spirit himself intercedes for us with groanings too deep for words. And he who searches hearts knows what is the mind of the Spirit, because the Spirit intercedes for the saints according to the will of God. . . . Who is to condemn? Christ Jesus is the one who died—more than that, who was raised—who is at the right hand of God, who indeed is interceding for us. (Romans 8:26–27, 34)

Believers can always grow in the area of praying. They need to learn to pray according to God's will rather than asking to make

their own life simpler or more prosperous. Believers often emphasize praying for others or maybe others praying for them. New
parents may have plenty of prayer requests to share with whoever
would like to hear them—for rest, health, travel, understanding,
and more.

Romans 8 explains that God is also praying for his people. Some
people are known as praying people. It is always awesome to get on
their prayer list. How much better is it to know that God is praying?
There are a few things about God's prayer that can encourage new
parents.

First, God's prayers are always according to his will. The Lord
taught his disciples to pray that the Lord's will would be accomplished on earth as it is in heaven. This request is first applied to the
one praying. When God prays, there can be full assurance that his
prayers are done according to his will. Even if God's will involves
hardship, believers know that his grace will always be sufficient.

Second, God's prayers are always made with full knowledge.
God knows people's hearts better than they do. People's knowledge
is incomplete. They would like to think their motives are pure or
their love is pure. In reality, people are often a mixed set of emotions, and they do not even know what is in the mix. When God
prays, he is able to know their hearts and his will while bringing the
two together.

Third, God's prayers are made passionately. Sometimes people
pray because something is weighing heavy on their hearts. Other
times, they pray out of duty or out of an attitude that cares just a
little. When God prays, the Spirit prays with groanings too deep for
words. These groanings represent communication within the God-
head that do not have proper expression in words. Yet these prayers
are vital for spiritual well-being.

God Works Out His Plan and Will

Paul encourages, "Therefore, my beloved, as you have always obeyed, so now, not only as in my presence but much more in my absence, work out your own salvation with fear and trembling, for it is God who works in you, both to will and to work for his good pleasure" (Philippians 2:12–13).

God is working. New parents have confidence that through life they have a gracious heavenly Father who continually works in their lives. Philippians 2 reminds them that they have the responsibility to work out their salvation. This does not mean that people have to earn their salvation, but rather they must live out the implications of salvation in their community. This is not a task that people must do on their own. Instead, God is also working.

Each individual has unique stories about God's working. Rob often gets asked how he changed careers from engineering to being a pastor. He studied engineering physics, and then he worked in technology consulting in the mid 1990s. The short answer is that God was working one step at a time to direct and encourage us in his good purposes and will. As God worked and as we attempted to follow his leading, we saw his plan God unfold in our lives.

We could say the same thing about our children. We mentioned at the beginning of the book that none of our three children were planned. God's will for our lives with respect to children was not neat and orderly. It involved periods of infertility, a miscarriage, and a belief that having children was no longer a possibility. The unfolding of God's plan revealed the joy of raising two boys and a girl each separated by about four and a half years. This is another expression of God's care. He proved that he cared each step of the way.

God Is a Rock, Fortress, and Strong Tower

The Psalms used vivid imagery to describe almost everything. The descriptions of God are no exception. We selected a few verses from three psalms to highlight the words *rock*, *fortress*, and *strong tower*. Those are words that in the ancient world would describe stability and security.

- "The LORD is my rock and my fortress and my deliverer, my God, my rock, in whom I take refuge, my shield, and the horn of my salvation, my stronghold" (Psalm 18:2).
- "I waited patiently for the LORD; he inclined to me and heard my cry. He drew me up from the pit of destruction, out of the miry bog, and set my feet upon a rock, making my steps secure. He put a new song in my mouth, a song of praise to our God. Many will see and fear, and put their trust in the LORD" (Psalm 40:1–3).
- "Hear my cry, O God, listen to my prayer; from the end of the earth I call to you when my heart is faint. Lead me to the rock that is higher than I, for you have been my refuge, a strong tower against the enemy. Let me dwell in your tent forever! Let me take refuge under the shelter of your wings!" (Psalm 61:1–4).

The Psalms were sung in the community to remind everyone of the promises of God and to encourage the community to be faithful to the Lord. In each case, the psalmist assures his reader that God provides stability. When there is financial, relational, or health instability, God is the place where people's feet can firmly rest.

Fortresses and strong tower were defensive structures for protection. If one could get to the fortress or strong tower, then there was a better chance for survival. Even when something comes into new parents' lives that seems stronger or more powerful than they can handle, they know that they have the Lord as the ultimate fortress. Nothing can penetrate God's defenses. That gives parents assurance that if trouble comes, it is with the full knowledge of the Lord and he will be with them and give grace to them for each step in the journey.

Believers can be encouraged as they embark on the journey of parenthood because God cares for them. God's care extends to the heavens. Parents can trust him with their lives and with the lives of their children. They can cast all their cares on him because they know that he cares for them.

Exercises

1. Discuss with your spouse ten ways that you have experienced God's care in the last year.

2. Pick one or two passages in this chapter that help you have confidence in God's care, and post them in a prominent place in your home.

3. Now that you have your list of ten ways you saw God's care in the last year, think smaller. Commit to talking to your spouse about one way you noticed God's care for you each day.

Conclusion

WE BEGAN THIS book by saying that this is a resource that we needed. Many of the passages of Scripture contained in this book were familiar to us before our first child was born. However, God's Word is not only rich for the mind, it is incredibly practical for the hands. We did not know all the ways that our faith, hopes, dreams, and character would be tested. The parenting journey, which we are still on, continually reveals cracks and weaknesses in our character. Our journey is showing where we have little wisdom and we are forced to grow and change. But we also hope that this resource has been helpful for new parents.

There is, we hope, a very encouraging mixture of biblical truth with practical (much of it personal) application. We want to know the truth and we want to know how to put that truth into practice.

The gospel changes everything. New parents may know that the gospel changes their relationship with Christ and their relationship with others. But that is not all. When new parents realize that the gospel impacts everything, they can start to see how it influences their approach to labor and delivery. New parents can learn something about labor and delivery from classes, books, or a few internet searches, but they need more than the physical facts. The relationship new parents have with their savior and with one another will largely influence whether labor and delivery is a joyful, gospel-centered experience.

The gospel impacts how new parents furnish their home for a new arrival. It impacts how they choose to handle those early days of life. It impacts the goals that new parents establish. It impacts the way they parent and their outlook on life. The gospel impacts how we view physical and spiritual rest. The gospel will shape how we handle our sexual desires, how we teach our children, and how we rely on the Lord because he cares for us.

We believe this journey of parenting is a special blessing from the Lord. Babies will give new parents many reasons to rejoice, many reasons to fear and weep, and many reasons to be dependent on the God who loves and saves.

Psalm 127:3, 5a says, "Behold, children are a heritage from the LORD the fruit of the womb a reward. . . . Blessed is the man who fills his quiver with them!"

Appendix A:
For Mentors

THANK YOU FOR being willing to mentor a couple through this material or to lead your small group through a study like this. We hope the Lord will use it in a special way. We thought it might be helpful for mentors to get a few of our thoughts about each chapter and how we would talk about it with a person we are mentoring.

Remember that the exercises at the end of each chapter are designed to give couples the opportunity to think about the concepts being presented. These exercises could be the starting point for a discussion as mentors help with this material. Do not be afraid, however, to go beyond the exercises. Each couple will have their own strengths and weaknesses. Each group will have their own needs. Our chapters serve as a starting place for the journey of parenting.

Chapter 1: We believe that there is a spiritual preparation for parenting much like there are other types of preparation. We believe that the joys, blessings, challenges, and disappointments in parenting will test the strength of a person's walk with Christ. In almost twenty years of ministry, we have seen some families embrace their gospel calling to live worthy and we have seen some families drawn by the cares of this world. Emphasize with proteges the importance of gospel blessings. Talk to them about their identity so that they will remember it at two in the morning when they want to be sleeping.

We do not know what readers will face, but when their identity is in Christ and their affections are set on him, then parents will not become arrogant over the joys of parenting or hopeless over the disappointments.

Chapter 2: A tremendous amount of energy must be invested in the care of a little one. In the process, it is easy to lose sight of one's spouse. We want to emphasize that not taking care of one's spouse is not only wrong before the Lord and each other, but that it will not lead to the long-term benefit of children. This chapter reminds your mentees that God created marriage, blessed it, and the expecting parents are welcoming an addition into a home that is already functioning well.

If the couple being mentored struggles in their marriage, then we encourage mentors to pause and counsel about the marriage. Just like a marriage exposes weaknesses that individuals often are unaware of, so a baby exposes weaknesses in marriages. If a couple is having marriage problems, then it is highly likely that the arrival of a baby will expose more issues.

Chapter 3: We place a very high value on the Bible. Because the Lord is a Good Shepherd, there are graces available to his children. God is present and working. Some ladies will be helped by learning breathing techniques, but they will also need to find rest in Christ.

Some deliveries are relatively short, others are not. Some ladies endure twenty-four-hour marathons followed by emergency C-sections. Some children are born without apparent physical concerns. Other babies are taken from Mom's arms to NICU. There is even a small section of rooms at our local hospital reserved for moms who lose their babies.

We do not know what will happen during labor and delivery, but we know we have a Shepherd watching over us.

Chapter 4: We believe that bringing a baby home is an exciting experience. It is also a time when it is possible to put more emphasis on physical things than the Lord. Caring for a baby includes far more than all the gadgets—caring for a baby is sharing the love of Christ.

Many ladies have some questions about nursing. There are lots of available options here and we encourage you to offer guidance, compassion, experience, but also direct her back to Romans 14 and explain that whatever decision she makes it should be for the glory of God.

This chapter also emphasized the role of the family and community. Some couples will have both in place. Other couples will have little community. We strongly encourage the couple to see the value and blessing of God's design for a loving community to contribute to and receive from.

Chapter 5: In order to help parents, we want them to see the value and importance of clear goals. God's Word explains what parents are trying to accomplish. The goal is not for the child to become a sports star or a ballerina. Parents are seeking to fulfill the mission God gave them. At times it is easy to allow the tyranny of the moment to move parents off their God-given goals. This chapter reminds parents that they are seeking to help their children know Christ and learn to live obediently for him. That mind-set can be established early. It might be helpful to ask proteges how they have experienced being pushed from the truly valuable by the tyranny of the urgent before children were involved.

Chapter 6: We all benefit from humility, encouragement, and dependence. That is true in many areas of life, not just parenting. We want our friends to acknowledge that they do not really know what they are doing. This will keep them humble enough to listen to the Lord and to one another. If parents are not listening to one another, then it is highly likely that the child will be caught in a game of tug-of-war.

Parents should also encourage each other. Because new parents are not sure what to do, it is easy to become discouraged or feel like they are a failure. These are moments where the parents can encourage each other.

We also believe that dependence is a crucial issue in all of life. If spiritual change is going to happen, then God and his power will be part of the equation. It might be helpful if you shared some of your experiences in how you needed to be humble, encouraged, and dependent in the early days of being a parent.

Chapter 7: In our years of teaching the young couples' class in our church, this material has resonated with many new parents. They know they are stewards. They are trying to work out how stewardship might work in their case. Some moms stay at home, others have six weeks off of a paid job, and some have twelve weeks off. We believe it is important to explain to parents some of their options to be good stewards. That stewardship will impact time, money, and their heart.

We mentioned that we scheduled our children, but you have your own experiences. It might help the couple to hear what you did, why you chose it, and how you would change it if you were to do it again. Remember, you are not just sharing facts about your life, but the biblical convictions that led you to your choices.

Please also be sure, as you are mentoring, to ask about their heart. What are their fears? Worries? Excitements? Answers to questions like these will often explain how well expectant and new parents are connecting the truths to life.

Chapter 8: We described the blessings associated with several stages in a baby's life. We believe it is easy to adopt a mind-set things will be better when the next stage comes. Life will be better when our child can walk; our child is potty-trained; our child can take a bath on their own. This is a dangerous path to take. It creates a habit of looking ahead without enjoying where you are. Instead, believers learn to give thanks in everything. One implication is appreciating all the blessings that come at different ages. As you are mentoring, ask them what things they are thankful for, what blessings they are anticipating, and ways they are celebrating God's blessings.

This is also the chapter where we started a conversation called "What happens if your child is not healthy?" We encourage you to help them see that every child has limitations just like every child has blessings. As parents, we enjoy all the blessings and we seek to provide care and support for their limitations.

Chapter 9: We are not sure why some dads think that parenting is the wife's responsibility. It seems to us in our ministry that even though more women are working outside the home, men still place the bulk of the parenting responsibilities on them. Maybe that struggle begins in the early days. If Mom nurses, then the bond between baby and Mom is very strong and Dad can feel somewhat useless. That is why we encourage new and expecting parents to have Dad involved in parenting from day one. We believe that when fathers are actively caring and making decisions, they own part of the parenting and see their role as important. Mentors should encourage new fathers to be active dads.

Chapter 10: When a family increases from two members to three members there are significant changes. It is possible that new parents will cling for their old life—even for a few hours. Their old life was full of flexibility. Now it is not. New parents need physical and spiritual rest, but sometimes they confuse selfish "me-time" for God-honoring rest. Please encourage your mentees that this is a struggle for men and women. It is a struggle even though you are caring for a precious life. We encourage you to discuss specific examples of how they might find rest in the midst of their plans. We also encourage you to discuss possible times when selfish "me time" might dominate their hearts. The good news is that through Christ they can learn some amazing lessons about God's power, about God's power working in their lives, and about how to care when they are tired. In many ways this chapter could describe one of the most important ways that these new parents need to grow in order to serve the Lord with the remainder of their life.

Chapter 11: Sexual intimacy can be difficult after a baby is in the house. Sex may be different after a baby than before, even after the appropriate time for healing. A baby may be distracting. It is possible that the sexual desires of the new dad and the new mom do not match. But the gospel speaks to that issue as well. It is here when a new mom and a new dad have a chance to demonstrate patience, kindness, proper use of words, and care for one another. Sexual intimacy is a journey, and this is another step in that journey. We encourage you to openly ask how the couple is doing in their physical relationship. We also encourage you to determine whether there are areas that need more focused and direct attention because sexual sin can often be devastating to a relationship.

Chapter 12: Both learning to teach and learning to discipline are hard. The principles sound easy enough, but the execution is another matter. We encourage mentors to talk about the various ways they disciplined, what methods they used, and what they would do differently if they had the opportunity. This chapter is a sampling for the future. This material will not be fully implemented for quite some time. There are other resources that could be helpfully consulted along the way. Remind proteges of the top resources.

Chapter 13: The last chapter of the book reminds new parents that God is their ultimate source of joy, satisfaction, encouragement, and help. Believers cast their cares on him because he cares for them. New parents run to his throne because they find mercy and grace there. Children are a blessing from the Lord, but parenting is not always easy. No matter what the Lord allows in life, his care, presence, and comfort provide what believers need.

Thank you for mentoring others through this resource. May the Lord use it for his honor and glory.

Appendix B:
Need for Jesus

THANK YOU FOR turning to this section of the book. We understand that not everyone who reads this material will share our same convictions. We believe, however, that we are duty bound to say that we believe this book is built on the foundation of a saving relationship with Jesus Christ. That relationship with Christ and all that it entails changes our values, sets our priorities, and serves as the motivation and power to live out the truths found in the Bible. A relationship with Christ is required in order to be a Christ-centered or gospel-centered parent. So what is this foundation?

The first part is believing the truth that you are what the Bible calls a sinner. You have acted in ways or failed to act in ways that honor the Lord.

> Romans 3:23: "For all have sinned and fall short of the glory of God."

Some people want to minimize it, act like sin is not a big deal, or compare themselves to others. But that is not what God does. God commands us to meet his standard, and everyone falls short.

To make matters worse, God tells us that the penalty for sin is death. This is not just a physical death, but a separation from God for all eternity.

Romans 6:23: "For the wages of sin is death, but the free gift of God is eternal life in Christ Jesus our Lord."

2 Thessalonians 1:6–8: "Indeed God considers it just to repay with affliction those who afflict you, and to grant relief to you who are afflicted as well as to us, when the Lord Jesus is revealed from heaven with his mighty angels in flaming fire, inflicting vengeance on those who do not know God and on those who do not obey the gospel of our Lord Jesus."

Romans and 2 Thessalonians explain the significance of sin and the seriousness that God places on that sin. Thankfully, God also sent his son, Jesus Christ, to suffer, die, be buried, and rise again.

1 Corinthians 15:3–4: "For I delivered to you as of first importance what I also received: that Christ died for our sins in accordance with the Scriptures, that he was buried, that he was raised on the third day in accordance with the Scriptures."

That would seem to suggest that everyone is a rescued, but there is one more element. Each person must decide whether they will believe in Christ's rescue.

John 1:12: "But to all who did receive him, who believed in his name, he gave the right to become children of God."

Romans 10:9–10: "If you confess with your mouth that Jesus is Lord and believe in your heart that God raised him from the dead, you will be saved. For with the heart one believes and is justified, and with the mouth one confesses and is saved."

Friends, confessing Jesus as Lord is accepting him as your master. It is his Word that guides you, corrects you, and encourages you. Not everyone believes with their heart. We have every reason to love him because those who receive him become his adopted children. We encourage you to confess your sin and place your trust in his death, burial, and resurrection for your salvation.

**A practical vision of Christ-centered marriage
that is realistic, hopeful, and actionable**

ROB GREEN

TYING
THE
KNOT

A PREMARITAL GUIDE
—— TO A ——
STRONG & LASTING MARRIAGE

Engaged couples need to learn to communicate well in the midst
of conflict and set expectations with finances, intimacy, and more.
Starting a family brings many of these challenges up again. Don't
miss the opportunity to revisit *Tying the Knot*, an eight-session study
on a gospel-centered approach to marriage. This transformative
resource will help couples move toward Christ in realistic, hopeful,
and actionable ways.

NEW GROWTH PRESS